AVAILABLE TRUTH

AVAILABLE TRUTH

Excursions into Buddhist Wisdom and the Natural World

BHIKKHU NYANASOBHANO

Wisdom Publications • Boston

Wisdom Publications, Inc.
199 Elm Street
Somerville MA 02144 USA
www.wisdompubs.org

Library of Congress Cataloging-in-Publication Data
Nyanasobhano, Bhikkhu.
  Available truth : excursions into Buddhist wisdom and the natural world / Bhikkhu
Nyanasobhano.
    p. cm.
  ISBN 0-86171-519-5 (pbk. : alk. paper)
  1. Religious life—Theravada Buddhism. 2. Human ecology—Religious aspects—
Theravada Buddhism. 3. Theravada Buddhism—Doctrines. I. Title.
  BQ7285.N83 2007
  294.3'42—dc22
                                        2006036945

11 10 09 08 07
 5   4   3   2   1

Cover designed by Rick Snizik.
Interior designed by Tony Lulek. Set in Diacritcal Garamond, 11/14.5 pt.

Printed in the United States of America.

Table of Contents

Preface   vii

1. Toward the Horizon   1

2. Sangha and Laity   15

3. Contemplations from the Highway   29

4. Alone Between Past and Future   43

5. The Ritual Element   55

6. Multiflora Rose   67

7. Two Bright States   81

8. Our Next Destination   93

9. February in the Hills   109

10. Desperation and Peace   123

11. Undeclared Questions   137

12. A Cold Day with Much Sun   149

13. Dust and Excuses   159

14. Investigations in the Evening   169

Preface

BUDDHISM, AS A SYSTEM of teachings about the purposes and means of wise living, is always open to questioners and explorers. We who search for explanations of birth and death, who hope for safety from life's perils, can search here freely and test what we find by paying attention to the sensations that flash through our own minds and bodies. Inside our houses, and out in our neighborhoods, and beyond in the fields and forests and endless complexities of the world, fruitful truth is available if we seek it in the right way. This book presents some ideas for seeking.

To understand Buddhism well we need to practice it—at least in a preliminary, exploratory way—to apply in our own lives its standards of behavior and its ways of looking at the world. But to practice rightly we need to learn what the Buddha actually teaches about the nature of the universe. Intuitions require good instruction, and doctrines need to be confirmed in daily living. To act nobly we need both intellectual nourishment and the experience of training our minds by our own effort.

When we set out to search for truths to believe and trust we cannot rely just on energy and enthusiasm without instruction. At the same time, we cannot rest contented just with a set of doctrines mulled over and memorized. There must be a harmonious intermingling of ideas and actions, of listening and investigating, so that, knowing what to look for, we come to understand the original teaching better and better. Happily, this is possible.

This book is written from the standpoint of the Theravāda, the "doctrine of the elders." It attempts both to give some basic knowledge of important Buddhist principles and to suggest ways by which we can investigate those principles within the immediate world of our perceptions.

Buddhist technical terms are given here in their Pāli forms. The quotations from the Pāli Canon are edited excerpts of translations published by Wisdom Publications and by the Buddhist Publication Society of Kandy, Sri Lanka.

To the Sangha and to all followers of the Buddha of this age and past ages who have given me instruction and inspiration I offer my gratitude, thanks, and respect.

Bhikkhu Nyanasobhano

1. Toward the Horizon

WAKING EARLY TODAY to a cool summer morning in the country, we find that for a little while the world does not descend on us with its usual frenzy. There is a pause, a sweet quietude in the air. As we bumble about the house, trying to figure out why this might be so and trying to get started on what we had meant to do today, small things around us begin to seem significant. Birds outside sing with a pleasant simplicity, breaking off after each phrase as if to allow us time to ruminate on the message. In the kitchen a spoon rings faintly against a dish like a notice of some imminent music, and even the familiar smells of breakfast float up to us as if they carry a meaning worth contemplating. Cool air surrounds us as we sit beside a sunlit window and eat, and when we move our hands the air moves, too, in rolling, silent currents. We feel strangely expectant and alive— not restless but simply poised to apprehend whatever wonders may appear.

It is the weekend once again, and various plans begin to come to mind, but dimly and unappetizingly. These are not what we are waiting for. We know there is much that we could do today that would be useful or amusing but in no way original or inspiring. Would it not be good, then, to escape habit for once and get out somewhere in the countryside before the old preoccupations start to agitate us again? Outside, a breeze is just starting to flow through the trees, and enough strength is coming back to this body to set out on a small adventure, if we are ready to be adventurous.

On countless mornings we have thought, idly, of how good it would be to overthrow routine, not just by taking a new route to work or school but by sailing out into the world with wholly new intentions, by pursuing some fine inspiration rather than the same tiresome desires. Yet such reflections have mostly slipped by ineffectually. We have resolved and postponed, wondered and forgotten. Will it be the same today? Let us get going right now, out into that distant terrain we have so seldom explored. Maybe a breeze of thought will come along to pick up and sustain our effort.

How slowly we wake, even outside in the cool air ringing with bird song. Heavy dreams, which have possessed us so long, will surely pull us down again if we do not exert ourselves; but wakefulness, it seems, is not just a matter of stretching muscles. Some stimulating idea that we have left behind must be recovered. What was it? We muse on this as we leave the house and head for empty spaces.

Out on foot on a rural road, we go hiking along as cheerfully as we can, watching the world around us growing brighter. When will an original truth at last appear as indubitable as this yellow sun? On one side there are pastures wet with dew; on the other, green forest on hill and valley and farther hill; ahead, rolling farmland indistinct in the sun's glare. All this country we have seen before, passed through often; but this morning a sensation of expansiveness and expectancy runs through us as we gaze around, trying to look or to sense farther and more truly than we have before. Will our fair mood be just another feeling that washes over us, anomalous and without effect, or will an answering swell of understanding arise?

Perhaps we are once again, despite our exercise, despite the deliberate thudding of our shoes on the road, just waiting for the world to start edifying us. Should we not find a way to act on our own behalf, to start learning from the signs of nature already strewn about? What was that thought, that shadowy inspiration we almost recall? It was not anything small and transient but some grand structure of ideas we had just begun to explore. Ah! Now it comes back, at least in part. Last night we were reading, bent over a book and absorbing ideas that flashed with surprising beauty. Things were beginning to make sense—

in a quiet, intellectual way, at any rate—and that was rare enough amid our usual hurry and agitation. We could see profound matters to pursue, profound matters to test. And then, of course, we got tired, and the evening at last dissolved into fatigue, confusion, and sleep. But something of our delight has not vanished; something has urged us out this far into the fragrant summer air. Let us therefore take up last night's contemplations and find out whether they can stand the daylight.

We stride this morning without any special destination down an unremarkable road among farms and woods—we who have a thousand urgent concerns about family, work, money, and health—and we are thinking, with more earnestness than usual, about Buddhism. That was what kept us up late and what lies behind our present feeling of expectancy. While we worked through the pages, doctrines, beautiful ideas, and ancient tales mixed together gracefully until we began to think, in the quiet and calm of late evening, that here indeed was a path of surpassing reasonableness and promise. It seemed worth testing—and it would need testing, for we knew that what pleased us in our secluded reflections might turn out wan and negligible amid the humdrum we mostly live in. We fear such a disappointment, so unpoetical is life in general, but the glaring morning demands investigation. If Buddhism as an abstract collection of ideas seems persuasive, that is fine, but how well does it fit with rough reality and how well does it prescribe how we ought to live for our true welfare and happiness?

Maybe we should first try to see whether what Buddhism says about the nature of reality is true—whether it describes well how things actually behave. Our senses are probably operating this morning as well as we can expect, so we should be able to start observing with some seriousness. Here is this body with all its complaints wobbling down a road. Here is a locust tree with a heavy green drapery of vines. Here are farmhouses, fields, horizons—the infinities and particulars of existence. What one true thing can be said about them all? This we remember well enough. One of the fundamental facts about the universe that Buddhism emphasizes is the fact of impermanence, the changeable and changing nature of everything we can perceive.

All phenomena, all formations, are impermanent *(anicca)*; they are mutable, transitory, subject to destruction; they do not last and cannot last. Changes, subtle or gross, are always going on; and although we might nod at this obvious truth, we might not have reflected much on its troubling corollary, pointed out by the Buddha, that what is liable to change is necessarily unstable and unsatisfactory. Small changes in the details of our household lives and colossal upheavals in nature both warn us, if we are attentive, of the certain dissolution, and thus the inadequacy, of our present comforts. If all things can change and do change, then we must look on the world with caution, for all of it is inherently unstable, unsubstantial, and ultimately unreliable.

But is the world really so impermanent? Now that we are out of our philosophical armchairs (where, if it pleases us, we might imagine almost anything), let us look around. Does anything around here stay the same forever? This human body that puffs along the road? That tree draped with vines? Look where you will. These orange lilies spilling over the roadside ditch—where were they a month ago? Where will they be come autumn? A breeze is blowing over the pastures and over us, but half an hour ago the air was still and sweetly stagnant. Now that we notice it, the dew is ceasing to sparkle on the grass. We like to feel, after the turmoil of the city, that the countryside remains placidly timeless; but over there a ruined barn silently manifests time, with its roof rusting through and the boards on its sides pulling away from the frame. Once it stood solid and new, now it decays by small but irrevocable degrees, and eventually it will be entirely gone, vanishing even from the memories of wanderers like us. In the meantime, we are passing a tidy new house on a freshly scraped square of earth. Here, not long ago, there was pasture or tilled field; and here, to be sure, some years hence, there will be bricks and rotten boards to clear away.

Suppose we were visiting this land in our old age, looking for signs of our childhood here—would we find anything unchanged? Great landmark trees have fallen; new houses have been built; the generations have scattered; no unaltered face, or no known face at all, would greet us. Against the light of morning we see myriads of small insects hovering over the fields; but their lives are appallingly short, and if next year we see them again in a golden light it will be only a pattern repeated. For human beings it is much like this. Change will be slow or fast, but change is certain.

We sense a grand timelessness in nature—which is one reason we like to wander out here, briefly free from our schedules—but it is a timelessness only of pattern, not of unique things. Processes run on in winds and suns and seasons, but we can detect no single thing, no fragment of reality, that preserves itself unchanged—certainly not this body of ours. As for this chattering, fretting mind—gnats against the sunlight show more substance. Material or mental, all compounded, formed, conditioned things flow on without pause. So Buddhism teaches; and the perceptible universe, in all its limbs and aspects, displays this truth when we observe mindfully.

A second fundamental fact emphasized in Buddhism follows from the first. This is the fact of suffering, or *dukkha*. What is impermanent, changeable, and changing is also unstable, unreliable, and prone to suffering. Worldly joys and comforts depend on at least a semblance of stability; to satisfy us, events must run continuously and peacefully in one desired direction. But they never do that for very long; they jolt, they alter, they disappear. So joys and comforts built on worldly things are necessarily brief, untrustworthy, and thus in a deep sense unsatisfactory. Even those most prized of lovely conditions—youth and health—turn out to be just impermanent states that naturally and grievously give way to old age, sickness, debility, and death.

This truth of *dukkha* is one that causes us to sigh, even on such a splendid morning with the temperature ideal and a radiant landscape all around and a nice breakfast inside us. We do not enter eagerly into a reflection on the extent of suffering in these circumstances; but as we step briskly along the empty road and notice the features of the land, we edge unwillingly toward troubling facts. Impermanence implies suffering. Health and safety cannot last; undesired conditions inevitably erupt into any life, even though we might avert our eyes and narrowly fix our thoughts on signs of beauty. These shrubs and flowers on the roadside, for example—when we pause with a more considering look we notice that their foliage has been half eaten away by bugs and caterpillars. At the same time, the birds that have been popping in and out of the weeds so cheerily are devouring those same hungry creatures. Parasites and diseases meanwhile afflict the birds, which sooner or later expire and drop unnoticed into the grass. Life wrecks life and succumbs itself in time. What shall we fairly call this situation?

How the mind shies away from disagreeable reality! Just a minute ago, did we not we pass a snake crushed on the road? We glanced, shuddered, and hurried on, adroitly forgetting, to admire vistas of clover far ahead. Such is our habit—natural, human, and understandable. The beauties of the world abound, undeniably, and they arouse a kind of wistfulness and spiritual longing, but when clung to they disguise the landscape of reality.

The third characteristic of existence is nonself—*anattā*. Whatever is impermanent, transient, changing—namely, all of this sensed universe— is consequently unsatisfactory and conjoined with suffering; and whatever is unsatisfactory, temporary, liable to dissolution, and conjoined with suffering is not a self; it cannot justifiably be deemed a self, ego, identity, or nucleus of our being. When we think of a self, we are thinking of a discrete, lasting essence, something within or behind us that does not change. In actual experience, rummaging through the aspects of our existence, we cannot discover any lasting essence. This doctrine of nonself is a startling teaching, one that may puzzle us when we first come across it, but one with rich and exhilarating depths. Could it be that we have all along mistaken the foundations of our existence and the fundamental assumptions out of which we reason? Could human life, and all life, be constructed in quite another way than we have imagined? So the ever-crumbling, transmogrifying nature of reality powerfully implies.

We must look again to our immediate experience. Farms and forests around us are changing, without doubt. This human body changes by the moment, grows hot or tired in an hour, and eventually gets sick and old and dies; and meanwhile this mind wavers dizzily, thought by thought. Because all these things change they necessarily manifest unsatisfactoriness—there is no real rest or stability within them. Where among them could we locate an ego or a self? Hand and foot, eye and ear, breath and thought cooperate for a while in the process of our living; but no element that we have yet discovered sustains itself unchanged and independent.

This universal characteristic of nonself, though counter to ordinary assumptions about sentient existence, is not problematical in any practical way. Life still functions; and it functions best, perhaps, when we are least disturbed by egoistic desires. Sometimes, indeed, when we wish to perceive some object accurately and completely, or to accomplish a piece of work with the utmost skill we have, the usual considerations of self or "me" recede from consciousness, and there remain only the intent watching, assessing, and striving of a concentrated mind. Time recedes, too, along with the trivial hubbub of the day. Forgetting or just disregarding our name and standing in the world, we remain for a little while lucidly attentive to what lies before us and thus better able to understand and deal with it than in more worldly moments. We have, it is true, seldom kept up such a calm, disinterested view very long, but the experience hints at possibilities. If all egoistic considerations could be abolished, not just suppressed, with what lightness and freedom might we then explore the world?

It is reasonable, surely, to pay attention to what is actually here. Sights, sounds, smells, tastes, touch sensations, and mental objects arise and pass away continually, and out of this ocean of sense experience we make up an image of the world. But if we misperceive and misunderstand these basic sensory events—if we insist on regarding them as permanent, substantial, and connected with ego—we will surely make up a faulty, misleading picture of reality. Through a skillful effort, might we observe without wrong presuppositions and so distinguish true shapes and meanings? Buddhism teaches us that this is possible. Here, perhaps, is where hope rightly begins.

Alone on the empty road in the now-breezy morning, we are free to drift along and gaze off at the mingled colors of distant fields or at the crowded patterns in grass nearby. Near or far, the land is a stir of perceptions as fluid as any sea. Have its currents bewitched us? By means of Buddhist teaching could we resist enchantment? These are possibilities that deserve, more than thought, energetic inspection.

Here the road runs on a stretch of high ground, from which we can stare off with pleasure into beautiful distances—the near forest with individual trees distinct, and then the next ridge, rich with textures and shades of green, and then vaguer hills and lowlands beyond that, where farms and subdivisions spread out and where we might indulge our dreams most pleasantly. Adventure, peace, and charm may be supposed to flourish there, far away, just beyond the last reach of our vision. If our vantage point were a little higher, we might get a better view still and take into our contemplation a greater swath of landscape with perhaps more beautiful and more inspiring elements; or if we were to set out walking or traveling by car we might pursue those unclear features out on the horizon and identify them without doubt. These notions appeal to us, especially now in the freshness and vigor of the summer morning; but realistically we have to remind ourselves that no greater understanding is likely to come from perceiving still more shapes vaguely in the far distance, and that even if we were to transport ourselves to the next hill or valley the magical would become again the prosaic, and the horizon would still swim out of reach.

There are limits to the range of our perception by eye and ear and other senses, and the universe beyond is nothing to us but a blurry suggestion of wider mysteries. Nearby, the landscape falls away in smallness, too. We contemplate the streaks of color on the lilies by the roadside, trying to find their source or basis, and if we stop and squint and shade our eyes just right, we can make out within a single blossom a thousand tiny lines and specks and networks of minutiae; but here, just as on that outer horizon, we quickly come to a limit we cannot pass beyond. Color and form microscopically shrink away from us into presumable infinity, until we have to blink and shake ourselves and sigh. Here we are again, human and limited, living within the small mortal circle of our powers.

Happily, a correct and useful understanding of the world does not depend on the gross range of our perception but on the accurate observation of what is available to us. The world we are aware of is just eye, ear, nose, tongue, body, and mind, together with their corresponding objects of sights, sounds, smells, tastes, touch sensations, and mental objects. The calm, unbiased apprehension of just these will give us the knowledge we need.

Reflecting on these principles of impermanence, suffering, and non-self, at the same time as we glance at tiny pebbles in the road or scan the huge horizon, gives us this morning a sense of confidence and inner momentum, as if the words in old books are at last uncurling into prodigious life. Of Buddhism as a religion, as a system of philosophy, we have perhaps known something; but Buddhism does not just explain but leads, urges, and opens the way for our own exploration. Not all adventures need be geographical.

But why, apart from curiosity and eagerness for exercise, should we be seeking and traveling at all? The Buddhist explanations of the three characteristics of existence themselves supply the reason: since all things that we know of are impermanent and sure to leave us, since old age, sickness, and death will certainly befall us, and since we have found no literal ego to delight in and take refuge in, then our human intelligence and strength, while they last, should surely be used to seek relief, safety, and a permanent freedom from all flawed conditions.

This is a grand and thrilling prospect. Such freedom was what the Buddha himself sought. All this doctrine, this ancient teaching that has now reached us, began with that one mortal man, Siddhattha Gotama, who through his own efforts became the Enlightened One, the Buddha. Doubt, pain, and the mysterious temporariness of life drove him out of a coddled, spurious security and into an ascetic struggle in the forests of India, where he finally triumphed over ignorance. What he came to understand at last through direct knowledge was that all things in this *saṃsāra,* this cycle of birth and death, rise and fall according to conditions in a beginningless, dynamic process of cause and effect. There is no permanence, no stability in this saṃsāra, only the driving on of impersonal conditions giving rise to all phenomena, good and bad, pleasant and painful.

For living beings the most significant fact of existence in this ocean of change is the presence of suffering or unsatisfactoriness *(dukkha).* Certainly there is much delight, pleasure, love, and joy in life, but all of that, no matter how wonderful, is shadowed by suffering because of its impermanence. This suffering is not an eternal certainty, however; it is not unavoidable; rather, it is a conditioned state brought about by causes.

The fundamental, primary cause or origin of suffering is, according to the Buddha, craving *(taṇhā)*. When there is craving, there follows clinging; and because things incessantly change, there always comes separation from what we desire and cling to, and that separation is unsatisfactory; it is suffering. But if we entirely eliminate our craving, the necessary condition for suffering is removed, and suffering ceases. This cessation is called *Nibbāna*—liberation, deliverance, supreme happiness—and it is what the Buddha himself understood and achieved. He also mastered a further profound truth: there is a way of behaving, of wisely and honorably living this mortal life, that leads to Nibbāna. This is the Noble Eightfold Path, whose factors are right view, right intention, right speech, right action, right livelihood, right effort, right mindfulness, and right concentration.

When the Buddha began to teach it was from the foundation of these Four Noble Truths: the truth of suffering, the truth of the origin of suffering, the truth of the cessation of suffering, and the truth of the way leading to the cessation of suffering. It is not knowledge alone, not indiscriminate knowledge, that we lonely, doubting seekers after happiness need, but direct understanding of these Four Noble Truths. We must see our mortal situation without evasion, acknowledging the implications of universal impermanence; and we must learn that this situation with all its liabilities and sorrows ultimately depends upon and is brought about by our own habitual error—most specifically, by craving.

Following the teaching of the Buddha further, we should come to understand that the great flow of causality can operate for our good as well as for our harm. If craving, instead of being indulged, is abandoned, renounced, set aside, and abolished, then the miserable state that depends on it—suffering—will certainly come to an end. It is purely a question of cause and effect. Removing bad causes and substituting good causes is then the practical work that awaits us along the Noble Eightfold Path. Enlightenment is a matter of intelligent and virtuous striving.

To be out this morning freely roaming through beautiful country is a fine thing, but how much finer it is now that we reflect, right amid the walking and seeing and smelling, on ideas of great intellectual beauty. Serious thought and the actual breathing and tasting of life should not stay separate. The Buddhist religion is only partly communicated to us through books; we have to carry its teachings out to expand in the sunshine and prove themselves under our testing eyes. This, it seems, is what we have already begun today, just by noticing the ravaged foliage beneath the flowers and suspecting the common mortality behind the liveliness of bees and robins. Remembering our revulsion at the dead snake, we frown and grow somber; but taking in the vision of those lovely, promising distances out there beyond the hills, we are lifted again. Suffering and the cessation of suffering—the vital subjects of the Buddha's teaching—are symbolized and evidenced throughout this amazing realm of our perceptions. Both the horrible and the sublime can contribute to our advancement when we see them in the light of well-taught principles.

These principles, doctrines, and explanations of wise conduct are together called in Pāli the *Dhamma* (*Dharma* in Sanskrit). Often the word is used simply to refer to the collected teachings of the historical Buddha, but Dhamma also and more generally means liberating truth, the nature of reality, and the way to enlightenment. It is contact with the Dhamma that allows us, who have been figuring and philosophizing all our lives, to make sense at last of what we perceive around us. Not only that, but the Dhamma is a reliable guide to wise action for our own good and others' good. Supported by a coherent description of the forces that operate in the world, our longing, our will, and our strength may at last move confidently in one direction—toward Nibbāna, the liberation from all suffering.

This morning in an hour of solitude we meet no cars on the road and we see no people nearby—only a few small figures working on a far hillside and others, still more remote, going and coming soundlessly between farm buildings in another quarter of the visible country. The growl of a tractor is audible for a few minutes then sinks away, while birds go on singing. Thinking about the Dhamma, we feel no need to hurry toward any figure, any object in the landscape; we just keep on hiking down the road at any easy pace.

Distance has advantages besides scenic pleasure. Looking from one farm to another, and on beyond to splotches of subdivisions and the minuscule roofs of a far-away town, we can contemplate the changing nature of things with something of a historical calmness, for we realize that we exist in the same vastness of possibility as any earlier generation. We can imagine life out there toward the horizon as dignified by time and striving, as long-abiding, free from squalor and pettiness. It is just an ideal, we know, but our capacity to sense such grandeur reminds us of the promise of our own existence. There is still, we see, scope for our aspirations; and with the Dhamma at last to guide us there is no reason to despair or sink to resignation. We might yet do fine deeds.

Distance, besides, fires us with hope for the unseen and the unexplored in the spiritual sense. A ripple of bird song barely heard from the green woodlands foretells the rising of nobler music out there somewhere in a possible and reachable world. On the horizon the last gray line of earth, losing all solidity, blends with the lowest clouds. That literal boundary we cannot reach, but it remains as metaphor and advertisement for a finer transition, still accessible to the dedicated seeker, from the coarse to the sublime, from bondage to release.

The road now begins to drop down a long ridge toward a valley, and we lose those tremendous vistas for a while, but with our thoughts now running eagerly over what we know of the Dhamma, skipping ahead of our feet, we feel no disappointment. Surely there are great realms of being to discover at every step. Here, for instance, is another old barn right beside the road—huge, doorless, paintless, pathetic, its sides covered with poison ivy. This ruin, like all ruins, serves very well as an emblem of impermanence; its decay bespeaks unsatisfactoriness; and its hollowness, its cavernous vacancy, calls to mind the egolessness of things. Our situation as mortal beings remains what it was, while this new life of Dhamma, as yet barely formed, surges within us. Under the sun's clear blaze we remember our sorrows. We remember our failings, our fears, our bleak desires. Having walked farther than we would have expected in this summer morning, having gladly crossed this small stretch of landscape, is it time to cross the wider wasteland of ignorance?

Now we have reached, perhaps, a reasonable point in our morning walk at which to turn and head back to the house. But even as we return to the worldly duties of the day, shall we not venture on into those profounder, spiritual distances we have glimpsed? From where we stand now, we look up a slope of deep grass as far as we can. It is just a hundred yards of wavy, uncut, green field, ending in blank blue sky. We cannot see over the crest. Does the earth finally end there? Would we behold from that height stupendous vistas of paradise or only more woods and ponds and cornfields? From the Dhamma we learn that all phenomena everywhere share the same fluttery, vanishing nature, so we cannot expect a passion for novelty to lead us anywhere except to exhaustion at last. But this field that runs up to a seeming heaven is still an emblem or an indicator of the untrammeled and wisely directed life that we might realize. Somewhere, if not in this specific landscape, the earthly touches the infinite, and toward that frontier, with a little more resolve, we might be traveling.

2. Sangha and Laity

WHEN WE READ TRANSLATIONS from the Pāli Canon, the great collection of early Buddhist scriptures, trying to get as close as possible to the teaching of the historical Buddha, we are, perhaps unconsciously, doing a sort of translation of our own. We are assembling in imagination scenes, stories, and conversations from what is to us a remote, exotic age and trying to bring their lessons through to our own time and cultural circumstances. Mostly this work goes on quite easily, because the Buddha's teaching, though it is very profound and complex in parts and sometimes makes reference to customs that are strange to us, is happily universal in its application. The Buddha deals with timeless matters of suffering and joy and good and evil. His words are clear, his logic is straightforward, and his meaning is beautifully accessible. We read and ponder and usually manage to get the essence into our own internal idiom, leaving behind such of the original narrative as seems irrelevant or too hard to understand. Often this process of selection and cultural translation seems to work all right, but not always.

The Buddha taught the Dhamma not as bare doctrine written down on pages but as advice, instruction, and explanation to living people with questions and needs—curious, hoping, worrying people of all classes and characters who were making a living, dealing with relatives, suffering or rejoicing in their own long-established society. They had deep backgrounds of family, clan, and country; they had religious traditions; they had customs and opinions and expectations. Few if any of these circumstances, obviously, exist unchanged in our society today, but if we ignore them entirely we will have a harder time in comprehending the Buddha's message.

One of the most important social differences between the Buddha's time and our own day—and the one that most bears upon our understanding of the Dhamma—lies in the prominence of the career of religious renunciation. To be a monk in northern India in the time of the Buddha was, though somewhat unusual, not terribly surprising. When the Buddha established his *Sangha*—his religious order of monks and nuns—there already existed a tradition of monasticism, asceticism, and religious withdrawal from conventional society. While most people remained all their lives as householders fully absorbed in worldly business, a certain number left the household life voluntarily, desiring to live simply, even very strictly, with their entire focus on religious practice. They were able to do this because society at large respected the ideal of renunciation and was willing to feed and clothe and otherwise support such persons. It was thought that gifts to philosophers, brahmins, religious ascetics, and monks would yield benefits both mundane and spiritual to the givers. It was also believed that the career of renunciation was in itself a great good, an unsurpassable opportunity to work for spiritual liberation, and that if one could not undertake it oneself, it was wise to honor and help those who could.

The institution of monasticism and admiration for renunciation and self-denial are hardly noticeable in the Western world today, and this fact may influence our attitudes when we first read the Pāli Canon or otherwise attempt to learn about Buddhism. Religious renunciation, although it still exists, is so obscure within our society today that it is barely conceivable for most of us as either an ideal or an actual career. We grow up having heard of monks, certainly, having some picturesque notions of bygone times, but probably never having seen a monk of any kind. To *become* a monk—to live observing celibacy and a whole system of disciplinary rules—is all but unthinkable.

When, therefore, we begin to study Buddhism, we enter in imagination into a world that seems, in some of its underlying conditions and assumptions, fantastic and incomprehensible. We are interested, quite naturally, in what will be relevant for us, what will inspire or protect us in our present circumstances, so we edit automatically; we translate the Buddha's meaning, as far as we understand it, into terms that, we think, suit better nowadays. This process can get out of hand, however, especially concerning the vital subject of renunciation. In order to get help from the ancient texts, we have to learn and keep in mind some facts of history as well as doctrine.

Skimming over the pages of the Pāli Canon, we can see that most of the discourses of the Buddha recorded there were addressed to monks. He was speaking, in most instances, to people who had already accepted the Dhamma and, much more than that, who had already taken the step of abandoning the household life in order to train in celibacy under formal disciplinary rules. The interests and aims of these people were very different from those of most lay people, so they required a particular sort of teaching. This explains the Buddha's daunting emphasis on continuous striving, destruction of worldly desires, elimination of attachment, and radical simplicity of life—all ideals that would most likely baffle the ordinary householder. The Buddha's most frequent listeners, the monks, had already, to one degree or another, determined within themselves to break with mundane attachments and work to attain Nibbāna, the liberation from all suffering, so they were ready to hear the Dhamma in its most rigorous form.

The ordinary lay person nowadays who reads these teachings without considering who is being addressed, and under what circumstances, might make the mistake of thinking that the Dhamma is just too demanding, too uncompromisingly ascetic, for him ever to follow. Or he might make the opposite mistake of thinking that the struggle for supreme liberation can be comfortably adapted to his own circumstances as a layman. Without understanding the institution of the Sangha, he might assume that all the blessings of the Dhamma are obtainable without giving up any of his habits and pleasures, and that the monastic life is by no means necessary and has little relevance to busy lay people nowadays.

To avoid such misconceptions we need to look at some historical material in the Pāli Canon. Soon after the Buddha reached full enlightenment, he reflected thus:

This Dhamma that I have discovered is deep, hard to see, hard to understand, peaceful and sublime, not within the sphere of reasoning, subtle, to be experienced by the wise. But this generation delights in attachment, takes delight in attachment, rejoices in attachment.
(Saṃyutta Nikāya 6:1)

The pervasive attachment that the Buddha saw around him suggested to him that human beings would find the profound truths of the Dhamma too hard to understand; but fortunately for us the Buddha saw also that there were some people with "little dust in their eyes" who would be capable of understanding. Out of compassion, then, he decided to teach.

The important question then arose as to whom the Buddha should first teach the liberating Dhamma. He thought first of his two former teachers, Āḷāra Kālāma and Uddaka Rāmaputta, who had long had but little dust in their eyes and who would have understood quickly; but as both of them had recently died, the Buddha decided to go to see the five ascetic wanderers who had attended on him during an earlier period of his striving. These five were—significantly—not ordinary householders or laymen with families and professions. They were *samaṇas*—ascetics, monks, world-renouncers—who had already left behind the lay life. They were the likeliest persons to understand what the Buddha had to communicate.

When the Buddha reached the place where these ascetics were staying and gave his first discourse, making known to them the Four Noble Truths and the Noble Eightfold Path, they did, in fact, one by one understand what he said, and each attained to *sotāpatti*—"stream-entry," the first level of enlightenment. Then each man—and this also is significant—asked to be accepted formally as a monk under the Buddha's authority. For them there was no thought of going elsewhere or returning to lay life or doing anything other than living as monks in a community directed by the Buddha. The way to full enlightenment had been made clear, and each man asked for the Buddha's instruction. To their requests, then, the Buddha answered with memorable words: "Come, *bhikkhus*. The Dhamma is well proclaimed. Live the holy life for the complete ending of suffering" *(Vinaya Mahāvagga, Khandaka 1)*.

Such was the ordination of the first five monks, and such was the beginning of the Sangha, the monastic order—a beginning, we can see, that followed directly from the first arising of true knowledge in the Buddha's disciples. The "holy life" *(brahmacariya)* to which the Buddha welcomed them was in the broadest sense a religious, virtuous life, but it was also an unequivocally monastic life, which was to be carried out for the highest of purposes: "the complete ending of suffering."

Thus began also the *sāsana*—the Buddha's message and hence Buddhism as an institution. It began with a monastic, world-renouncing community of monks *(bhikkhus)* whose goal was not just social harmony or individual contentment in the present life but rather the complete, magnificent cessation of all suffering—Nibbāna. The achievement of that goal was the task of the individual; but a person who wished to approach that goal by the shortest route would need the wise companionship, spiritual discipline, and mutual help of a monastic community withdrawn from worldly distractions. The Buddha organized this community, the *Bhikkhu Sangha,* instituted rules for its governance, and saw to it that it would provide the best environment in which to carry on the great work of mental development. Some years later, when he established an order of nuns, the *Bhikkhunī Sangha,* it was according to the same method and with an aim toward the same sublime goal. There was no lessening in his emphasis on striving. All men or women who were accepted for training were expected to work not just to get along respectably in this life but to achieve complete liberation from saṃsāra, the cycle of birth and death.

From its earliest days the Sangha had to depend, like the other ascetic groups of the time, on the food and other support voluntarily given by lay people; and if lay people were going to respect the members of this new order, feed them regularly, and supply them with robes, medicine, and lodgings, they had to see for themselves that these monks were behaving well, that they were disciplined, modest, sincere, and energetic in their practice. Thus there had to be structure and formality in the order. What held together the Sangha in practical terms, and what gave it its distinctive, visible character, was at first the personal authority of the Buddha; but gradually, as the Sangha grew and dispersed over the land, the Buddha established the *Vinaya,* the great body of monastic rules and procedures that would enable the Sangha to carry on in his absence. The Buddha did not simply compose a set of rules at the outset of his career but rather announced rules one by one over time when monks violated unspoken principles or otherwise misbehaved, or when it became necessary to set up procedures for dealing with the many problems and details of communal life.

The Vinaya applied only to the ordained Sangha, not to the lay people, yet much of its content was concerned with the monks' relationship with lay people. Because the Buddha was very vigilant not only about the internal workings of the Sangha but also about its connections to wider society, when lay people complained about the conduct of monks he listened to them and often made rules to correct problems. Obviously the Buddha wanted the Sangha to present an inspiring image to the world and show itself worthy of material support, but he also wanted ordinary householders to partake of the blessings of the Dhamma. To do that they would first of all have to see the Sangha as worth listening to and worth looking to for advice and moral example. Thus the Buddha was careful, in teaching the monks how they should behave, to make sure that there would be a close, indeed daily, contact with the laity, and that the monks, while abstaining from all worldly business themselves, should rely on the good will of the laity for their livelihood.

In keeping with the tradition of the time, monks were to depend on the gifts of householders for their basic requirements; but the Buddha went further by requiring the monks to rely *only* on the householders—not setting themselves up independently, not withdrawing from contact with the rest of society. Monks could not take up worldly professions, could not accept gifts of gold, silver, and money, could not buy and sell, and could not engage in agriculture, for those would be ways to become self-sufficient and materially independent. Even in the matter of food the Buddha made surprising stipulations. Monks were to finish all meals for the day by noon, and they could not eat again until the next dawn. This rule acted as a check on gluttony, saved time for study and meditation, helped to prevent evening drowsiness, and kept the burden on generous lay people from becoming too heavy. In addition, the food itself had to be directly offered to the monks by a lay person—monks could not just take whatever they liked—and this offering had to be done every day. Monks normally obtained their food by wandering with their alms-bowls in the morning in the streets of towns and villages, accepting whatever food was offered, but they could also accept invitations to meals in the houses of donors. All meals were gifts to be eaten on that single morning only—monks were not permitted to keep food to use past that time.

To us today, who live in a society that prizes self-sufficiency and convenience, these rules seem puzzling at first, for they seem to make the monks extremely dependent on the laity. That, indeed, is exactly true, and exactly according to the Buddha's wise purpose. While his deepest teaching was directed to the Sangha, the Buddha did not forget the lay people, and by the rules he made he ensured a close, constant, and mutually helpful relationship. Since the monks had to receive their food as gifts every day, they certainly had to behave well. If they did not, if they offended their benefactors, they might not get fed at all, for nobody *had* to feed them—it was an entirely free and voluntary practice. Moreover, when wandering from house to house in the morning and waiting for whatever scraps someone might be pleased to give, the monks were reminded of their dependent status and their obligation to the rest of humanity. This way of getting food was a great inducement to humility, gratitude, and conscientiousness.

For the lay people the relationship was beneficial in several ways. They had the opportunity (and it was just an opportunity, not a requirement at all) to do a morally good action every day, if they wished, simply by dropping a bit of food into the bowl of a monk. It was not costly or troublesome, and it was a concrete help to the Sangha and a spiritual satisfaction for themselves. Such an action of giving was just the sort of thing, according to the Buddha's teaching about action and result, that would bring abundant benefit to the donors. Furthermore, with monks wandering through the villages every morning, lay people were able to observe them, to get to know them, to be reminded of the religious life, and to hear from them something of the priceless Dhamma. When people discovered that their gifts were useful and appreciated, that their opinions mattered to the Sangha, and that the monks were glad to teach them and help them with their doubts, they were naturally pleased and inspired. They became part of the benevolent, liberating tradition that the Buddha was spreading in the world.

Since those early days when the Buddha first set himself to his compassionate task, incalculable changes have occurred in human society, but the Sangha is still here, and the Vinaya is still here and still in force, and because of these facts the Dhamma is still available to seekers. The rules, standards, and procedures that the Buddha instituted have proved their worthiness over these many calamitous centuries by shoring up frail human will and keeping the way to enlightenment open to many. We who have happened upon the teaching of the Buddha, who have by chance picked up a book or attended a lecture, owe our excellent fortune directly to the Sangha and the faithful lay community that supports it. Even though we may have never laid eyes upon a monk, our introduction to the good Dhamma has been the result of the steadfastness of monks and the charity of laymen over many generations.

This introduction to the Dhamma, however, is only a beginning, not any kind of culmination or fulfillment. We cannot assume that, having plenty of books in front of us, we are now comfortably supplied for our pilgrimage to enlightenment and need not trouble ourselves with history or with a Sangha we have never seen. It is because of the dedication and discipline of the Sangha that the Buddha and the Dhamma are known to us at all today, and it is in the living Sangha that we can find visible, encouraging examples of principles of striving and renunciation taught by the Buddha that would otherwise remain abstract and far away. Thus, as we read our books and as we try to find our own place in Buddhist tradition, it is very useful to learn more about the monastic order and consider what our relationship with it should be.

Throughout the Pāli Canon we find, in addition to the emphasis on renunciation, a complementary emphasis on giving *(dāna)*. It is a wonderful thing when someone is sufficiently inspired to seek to become a monk or a nun; but it is also a wonderful thing when out of faith a lay person donates robes, food, medicine, lodgings, and other useful items to the Sangha. Certainly such donations are always necessary for the survival of the Sangha, but we today who have grown up without any relationship with monks at all are likely to overestimate the material aspect of this giving and notice only the advantage for monks. The Buddha, however, was compassionate and benevolent toward all beings, and that is precisely why he urged the performance of acts of charity. Giving produces lovely results for the giver; it is simply a function of the law of action *(kamma)* and result *(vipāka)*. When we give to a virtuous person, moreover, the result of that action is especially significant. A person who has renounced the household life and is living faithfully according to the Vinaya, striving honestly to overcome his defilements and reach enlightenment, is the sort of person who deserves support and to whom we can happily give, knowing that our actions will be very good for us, too. Buddhist tradition has long held, in fact, that when a monk goes out on his alms-round, quietly collecting food in the morning, he is actually conferring a blessing on people by giving them the chance to give and to be glad and to gain merit.

But beyond gifts to individual persons—who will naturally vary in their spiritual qualities—the Buddha praises gifts to the Sangha as a whole, saying that no gift to an individual ever surpasses a gift to the Sangha. At its very highest, when composed of genuinely enlightened persons, the Sangha is what the Buddha calls "the unsurpassed field of merit for the world." Even if, as is likely, the monks in some locality are not enlightened at all, and are not especially learned or talented or impressive, but are just honorable and decent monks, gifts to that Sangha are well worth making, for the Sangha is not only a collection of people striving to become better but also a symbol of enlightenment, community, and mutual help that edifies and beautifies society.

The Sangha gives to the layman various kinds of special, spiritual help that cannot easily be obtained from secular sources. In particular, the celibacy of the Sangha serves as a salutary example to the layman bewildered by sexual desire. Where else is there such self-restraint? What might these monks know that makes them give up the pleasures that all the world adores? What better and more beautiful goal can it be that they pursue? Such are the useful questions that may move even an entirely nonreligious person to a more serious examination of the purposes of his or her life.

As strictly celibate world-renouncers, monks are required by the Vinaya to be very circumspect in their relations with women. They must not only refrain from overt improprieties but must also avoid all dangers to their mental peace and to their reputations that might come about from too-familiar association with women. Visitors to Buddhist temples who are accustomed to the casual intermingling of men and women in ordinary society might be surprised at the reserve of monks and think they are being haughty when in fact they are simply trying to preserve a polite, tactful atmosphere in which everyone will be at ease. Most notably, monks are prohibited from sitting alone in secluded places with women. This wise rule certainly helps to protect the celibacy of monks, but it also benefits the laity by allaying mistrust and preventing ugly suspicions. If a monk is to teach or counsel a woman it must be done quite openly and with another man present. When everybody understands this and other rules and traditions that the Sangha observes, and when a mutually respectful distance is maintained, advice can be asked for and given without awkwardness or worry. Among well-disciplined monks the atmosphere is peaceful and secure for everyone.

Another important reason for paying attention to the Sangha is that to guide our actions we need to acquire wisdom, and in the company of ascetics is the best place to look. Simply in asking sensible questions there is great benefit:

> But here, student, some woman or man visits an ascetic or a brahmin and asks, "Venerable sir, what is wholesome? What is unwholesome? What is blameable? What is blameless? What should be cultivated? What should not be cultivated? What kind of action will lead to my harm and suffering for a long time? What kind of action will lead to my welfare and happiness for a long time?"... This is the way, student, that leads to great wisdom; namely, one visits an ascetic or a brahmin and asks, "Venerable sir, what is wholesome?"
>
> (Majjhima Nikāya 135:18)

Wisdom, we should understand, is not some nebulous, causeless aura but a natural power that arises based on conditions. Asking intelligent questions of accomplished persons is a practical way of setting up good conditions.

Another, subtler thing that for centuries has made the Sangha so important to lay Buddhists, and should make it important to us, is that human nature requires the comfort of seeing and knowing worthy people. Words, ideas, and art may move us; the Dhamma discovered in a book may start us thinking and groping after enlightenment; but we always need and yearn for inspiration in the flesh. We especially want to meet those who are more dedicated and disciplined than we are and who not only can teach us but can also show us a noble way of living. We benefit by hearing direct instruction, and we also benefit by being in the company of those who actually try to abide by the ancient, noble discipline we have read about.

Even though we may be lay people with dozens of mundane commitments and duties, and even though we may have no wish to renounce the world ourselves, it is yet uplifting and satisfying to have something to do with good monks or nuns. Apart from the actual Dhamma teaching we may receive, we get a flavor of the sublime; we are reminded of the possible depth of the religious life; we are brought to question our purposes and ideals and to consider whether we are striving for the right things. Harried and hungry as we usually are in the secular realm of business, money, and pleasure, the sight of true ascetics helps us to calm down and gives us spiritual nourishment. Their example emboldens us to think that we might actually get free of some of those burdensome pleasures that we have begun to doubt but that everybody else seems to think so vital. If monks and nuns can live peacefully without relentless entertainment, maybe we could do the same or at least begin to put aside unnecessary and wearying distractions.

As we gradually discover more meaning and beauty in the teaching of the Buddha, we may realize that a living, strictly-practicing monastic order is essential for the survival of the good Dhamma in the world and could give great help and inspiration for our own spiritual efforts. We can learn the basics in solitude, certainly; we can undertake wholesome Buddhist practices on our own; but over time we may feel somewhat deprived unless we have some contact, however slight, with the Sangha. While the fevered world of passion is always running, dissolving, flying past us in forms that never hold together long, the Sangha quietly keeps to its original ways, preserving the timeless Dhamma for the happiness of many.

It would be good, then, to look upon monks and nuns not as relics or negligible eccentrics of no use nowadays but as essential representatives of a noble tradition and sources of precious knowledge. If they behave properly, devoting themselves to the Dhamma and observing the Vinaya rules, they deserve support. In supporting such persons we are not merely doing acts of indifferent charity but are also powerfully benefiting ourselves and helping to keep the Dhamma available for our own and future generations. The Sangha is an institution that cannot do its work of spreading and exemplifying the Dhamma—cannot exist at all—without the help of the laity. Monks require food and lodging—who will supply these? This is something to be considered by anyone who wishes to benefit from contact with the Sangha.

When we meet with other people to listen to teaching monks and to offer food and other support to the Sangha, we enter into the Buddhist tradition ourselves and begin to alleviate our spiritual loneliness with good friendship. The deeper doctrines and the austerities of ancient times become less strange, and we come to realize that the way to final enlightenment, although it is not as easy as we might have once assumed, is a way that can indeed be followed in our own time. This is an encouraging thing, a happy thing to discover. For lay men and lay women and monks and nuns it is always the same Noble Eightfold Path, and we are all faced with the need to follow this path in order to overcome suffering and achieve happiness.

Although we might not be inclined to take up the rigorous monastic career ourselves, we can certainly find instruction and encouragement in the example of others and thereby partake of the blessings of the Dhamma. When we actually see renunciation being practiced in the customs and rules of the Sangha, we may get some ideas about how our own over-heated, over-complicated lives might be made cooler and simpler. The Buddha, explaining proper conduct in the monastic life to his aunt, the first bhikkhunī, gives some excellent principles that can serve today to guide monk and nun, lay man and lay woman:

Gotamī, those things of which you know, "These things lead to pas-sion, not to dispassion; to attachment, not to detachment; to amass-ing, not to dispersal; to many wishes, not to few wishes; to discontent, not to content; to association, not to seclusion; to laziness, not to the arousing of energy; to being difficult to support, not to being easy to support," of them you can quite certainly decide: "This is not the Dhamma, this is not the Vinaya, this is not the master's teaching."

But Gotamī, those things of which you know, "These things lead to dispassion, not to passion; to detachment, not to attachment; to dis-persal, not to amassing; to few wishes, not to many wishes; to con-tent, not to discontent; to seclusion, not to association; to the arousing of energy, not to laziness; to being easy to support, not to being diffi-cult to support," of them you can quite certainly decide: "This is the Dhamma, this is the Vinaya, this is the master's teaching."

(Vinaya Cūḷavagga, Khandhaka 10)

Such are the principles behind the formal rules for the Sangha, prin-ciples that the monks and nuns are to bear in mind even in cases for which no specific rules have been laid down. For Buddhist lay people, who are not bound by the Vinaya, these principles are also very useful and worthy of respect. They point onward to Nibbāna, and they suggest the kinds of attitudes we should develop even in the midst of our mun-dane business. Certainly from the earliest days the Buddha understood that lay people would generally not be attracted to the strictest form of renunciation as embodied in the celibate, monastic life, but that a whole-some and beneficial form of renunciation could still be practiced in lay life. It is a matter of drawing back from negligence, pleasure-seeking, and worldliness as well as we can, and cultivating such qualities as detachment, simplicity, contentment, and energy.

The devout layman of the Buddha's time, though he might not wish to become a monk himself, understood as a matter of course the idea of renunciation and understood the merit in the monastic career. Thus he was inclined to respect ascetics, brahmins, monks, and world-renouncers in general and was even more inclined when he saw Buddhist virtues exemplified in the persons of the bhikkhus and the bhikkhunīs. We today, who learn of the Dhamma distantly, through books, and have little or no contact with the Sangha, undertake our religious practice at a disadvantage that can and should be overcome. Immersed in a world that is secular, sensual, undisciplined, and heedless, we have to exert ourselves to understand, first, that a nobler life is indeed possible in our day, and second, that it can only come about through renunciation and dedication to timeless virtues. We can surely do more than we have done. A study of history will help, and, whenever we get the opportunity, the sight of good ascetics and respectful attention to the Sangha will help.

How strange it is to shave one's head, to wear the ochre robes, to forswear what the world covets. How strange to take on, without compulsion, an ancient discipline. Seen or only imagined, the Sangha is still to us a brilliant mystery, one full of blessings yet to be realized. Thinking over what has gone before us, thinking over the history of Buddhism as it grew in other lands, we should see that our search for peace need not be as lonely as it has been. Let us read, by all means, but let us take up good tradition, too, and live it honorably.

We have already had great good fortune, for the Dhamma has reached us through all the confusion and mischance of history; and now, it may be, we are eager to hear more and to enter into a life of more dignity and beauty. This can be done, and help can be found. Somewhere monks pass along a road in silence, in slow files or one by one, carrying their alms-bowls from house to house. Long ago they walked thus, and still they go on. Perhaps they will come this way.

3. Contemplations from the Highway

O N A GRAY AFTERNOON late in the year a few friends climb into a car and drive out into the country with much chatter and laughter and shaking of maps. After long weeks of busyness and fatigue in our usual routine, we are glad to be going, too, bound for a social gathering at the house of other friends an hour or two away. Fortunately, somebody else is doing the driving, so we relax into our seat, chat amiably, and watch the familiar scenery run by until, in a little while, it is familiar no more, and we are sailing out at ease over the great, strange earth.

It is an overcast day at the bedraggled end of autumn, but it is unusually warm, so the windows in the car are partly lowered, and the breeze flaps over us with the pleasing scents of soil and vegetation. The autumn colors have mostly fallen away from the trees, but still the landscape here and there preserves some tinges of red and yellow, and we delight to sit here swaying and looking out over woods, creeks, and chopped-down fields. Almost forgetting our usual business and our customary sorrows, we take pleasure in imagining ourselves entirely free—just vagabonds wandering away on an infinite adventure. The inexhaustible country rushes toward us and away too fast to absorb with any precision, but that hardly matters; it is enough to watch the grand flow of color, to smell the land, and to feel the invigorating impact of the wind. We might be going anywhere; we might be leaving all sorrow behind us forever.

After a little while we find ourselves only intermittently concerned with the conversation in the car; we are content just to sit here comfortably among friends, putting in a word now and then. Mainly we are drawn toward the ever-varying spectacle outside the window, the pageant of farms, small towns, subdivisions, factories, woods, and ponds. Our route is an old highway we have not traveled on for years, if ever, one that winds about and dips and rises with a pleasing conformity to the shape of the land. Beyond knowing the names of a few towns, have we ever been aware of this rural stretch of country? Effectively it is new to us; and while we enjoy the surprises looming up with each hill and valley, we cannot help wondering at a certain negligence within ourselves. Apparently we have been living in an insular and oblivious way, grinding away on our personal problems as if no connection with the greater universe mattered. Perhaps it does matter, though. We find now a new and zestful feeling in contemplating this life out here in the countryside, irrespective of the sorrows and enthusiasms that dominate our days. Billboards, stores alongside the highway, houses on distant hills, gas stations, warehouses, schools, people on sidewalks, harvested cornfields, gravel roads vanishing into the hollows, trains thundering away over the country—all these carry us in some sense out of ourselves and further into a region of possibility and adventure.

Mostly we have sought to dispel our problems by an earnest inward focusing, by poring over our private thoughts and moods; so it is interesting to notice that peace of mind seems to increase in these moments when our attention turns outward, or perhaps when we start to observe both internal and external things with more detachment and with less of our usual self-absorption. Crows hopping in the cornfields and dogs romping on rural lawns are surely living, intending, and acting with as dear a regard for their own welfare as we have for ours. Have we ever before paid much mind to the fact?

Now we are beginning to take a more careful view—just a swift and easy darting of attention from this to that brief evidence of life and longing. A child riding a bicycle up and down a driveway dwells in a reality as intense and wondrous as our own. We fly past in a second, but the picture registers. A woman is raking leaves in her yard while a toddler watches. A man rolls a tire in front of a garage. Two boys toss a ball in a vacant field. We glimpse a hundred vignettes and pass by, imagining histories, dramas, adventures behind these figures. It is humbling and oddly refreshing to realize, simply from our own calm watching, that after all we are not unique, that innumerable fellow beings wander through the cloudy afternoon and brood on their own griefs and hopes. We cannot doubt that they look as wonderingly as we do at the autumn colors falling and fading.

The question now arises as to how we ought to regard these living beings whose stories and thoughts we whimsically guess at. Perhaps it is the gray, ethereal nature of the day through which we fly, or the temporary detachment we gain by traveling thus—separated from the world yet close enough to observe with charity—but we feel a certain willingness now to entertain this question of our duty or our opportunity with respect to the living beings around us. We know from the teaching of the Buddha at least the rudiments of how we ought to *behave* toward other beings—what standards of honesty and consideration we ought to follow in our daily dealings—but what about our thoughts, our private attitudes, our inclinations that inscrutably come and go? How far should we try to reform or govern those?

The Dhamma, we know, is rightly understood as the means for achieving liberation from the cycle of birth and death and suffering, a means to be employed consciously and diligently by each individual for his or her own highest good. But the Dhamma is also the means for the betterment of our surroundings right here in this imperfect, mortal world; and our own good ultimately cannot be separated from that of others.

The Buddha recommends the cultivation of four "divine abodes" *(brahmavihāras)*. These are four wholesome states of mind developed beyond occasional, kindly emotions into sustained, powerful contemplations that range outward to encompass unlimited multitudes of fellow beings. The four are loving kindness *(mettā)*, compassion *(karuṇā)*, altruistic joy *(muditā)*, and equanimity *(upekkhā)*. To what extent, let us consider, have we established these qualities within ourselves? We might today or any day become conscious of feelings of amiability, kindness, pity, and the like toward particular people or animals. We might, when sufficiently moved, feel a diffuse good will toward the whole of humanity or even all earthly life. We might at times wish for more forbearance and good temper in our relations with others. But in order to make these occasional sentiments become "divine abodes," we have to work; we have to arouse, develop, and concentrate the good qualities that are, let us hope, at least latent within us.

How strangely the sights, sounds, and smells of the countryside bring us around to these reflections. Perhaps there is something in the sheer apprehension of land and age and distance that favors the birth of kindly imagination. We rush for a time over great lonely spaces under the gray sky, where we might believe that all strength and conviviality have vanished; and then a tiny house appears, and somebody is working or playing there; and when we see a few isolated figures thus in motion in the vastness of saṃsāra, a warmth of sympathy starts up in us. They become for us emblems of mortality and longing, starkly standing out for our contemplation; but they are also real beings whom we now perceive as not different in any fundamental way from us. For a moment or two, perhaps, we wish them well—consciously and intently—and this is what is meant by loving kindness. It is for us now, as it usually is, a passing impulse—but why must it pass? Would it not be good to extend it, make it stronger, make it part of our character? While we are inspired by loving kindness our dreary self-centeredness decreases, and the sensation, when we notice it, is pleasant and uplifting. If this sensation, or better this *activity* of mind, were made steadier, made more comprehensive, might we not feel better yet? Then, rousing a healthy force of good will, might we not see about actually doing those good deeds we often think we should be doing?

The Buddha says that when meditation on loving kindness is developed, ill will is abandoned. What hampers us in our quest for liberation from suffering is probably not so much a lack of intelligence or strength as the presence within us of defilements. Ill will is one such basic defilement, a contaminant of the mind that foils virtuous intentions and diverts us from the right path. Most of us are quite aware of this defilement; we regret it and worry about it and try to keep it out of sight; but, knowing no way to get rid of it, we have mostly resigned ourselves to enduring it. This is unsatisfactory, for the means of dealing with ill will are available.

Loving kindness is the specific antidote to ill will; it opposes that defilement and, if properly exercised, drives it away. It is important and encouraging to understand that in Buddhism loving kindness, like other wholesome reflections, is not a passive emotion, not just a response to some fortuitous experience, but an intentional activity of the mind, an initiative carried out to promote our own and others' welfare. We should not sit around and *wait* until exceptionally pleasing circumstances cause us to beam upon our neighbors; rather we should arouse loving kindness by our own will, extend it, expand it, and apply it near and far.

Very soon in any study of Buddhism we come across this consistent principle of action, this idea that we should learn the essential causes for good and worthwhile states and then pragmatically set about obtaining them, let the willy-nilly world do what it may. Cause will launch effect— of this we can be sure. If we notice that when loving kindness occasionally blossoms within us it soothes us and soothes others, that it suppresses the fires of ill will, that it calls up good cheer all around, then surely we should consider the advantages of more deliberate cultivation.

The Buddha teaches his monks to develop loving kindness both for their own spiritual advancement and for the benefit of their community. That loving kindness, in order to become complete and efficacious, must express itself in all the three ways of action—by body, speech, and mind:

> *Here a bhikkhu maintains bodily acts of loving kindness...verbal acts of loving kindness...mental acts of loving kindness both in public and in private toward his companions in the holy life. This is a memorable quality that creates love and respect and conduces to helpfulness, to non-dispute, to concord, and to unity.*
>
> (Majjhima Nikāya 48:6)

If contemplation of the living beings we glimpse in our travels today arouses a vague benevolence in us, that is fine—we get at least the flavor of the divine abode of loving kindness. But we can see from the teaching of the Buddha that much more self-discipline and work are required to get the best results.

Loving kindness is not the only important quality we should develop with respect to others. As we sit here in the car, rocking and bumping over the miles, we are reminded by signs around us of the undesirable conditions that living beings must endure. The immensity and age of the land and the huge, helpless grayness of the sky seem to emphasize the frailty of all life, its brevity, and its pitifulness. Above small living creatures a cold power of nature always impends. The breeze, still warm today, will soon whip down the valleys with the freezing winter. As it is, thin showers of leaves are streaming away dismally from the woods, leaving the landscape gradually more somber. Looking into and past this grave beauty, we reflect on our sorrows; we imagine sorrows behind the faces on the porches and the sidewalks we pass, sorrows multiplied in the persons of innumerable beings who all, as they partake of air, partake of misfortune in this ambivalent realm of existence. A cool and distant sadness touches us, but there is another sensation stirring beneath that, one that becomes more definite the more we brood on particular signs before us.

Now a treeless cemetery slides by on one side, a drab acre with withered flowers on a few—only a few—headstones. We notice one particular spot of color and realize that somebody trekked out there, unheeded, and propped up a little bouquet that seems to us now just an emblem of pathos. Do the flowers in that cemetery become fewer over the years? Or do new burials faintly renew the custom? We turn to look longer, pondering—but the scene is behind us. Now we are slowing through a small town, and there in front of a house stands an ambulance with the lights on. A door in the house opens and we glimpse some bustling figures—but quickly we are away, we are past that, coasting by vacant, decrepit stores on whose dusty windows the lettering is flaking away. That scene, too, falls behind us; but in a little while, as our gaze swings here and there, lighting on individual forms and faces, we become aware of a grave and gentle feeling that we might fairly call compassion.

While loving kindness is a warmth of plain good will extended toward beings, compassion is a feeling of sympathy for the sorrows, losses, and misfortunes of others, and as such nothing more than a humane response to suffering outside ourselves. As a divine abode, however, it is a universal, unbiased, and unlimited sentiment, a selfless pity and concern.

Like loving kindness, compassion is also an activity. We experience it at first, perhaps, as a kindly reaction to some particular living being's distress; we are moved to consider suffering as an important and troubling fact even when we do not feel it personally; we are further moved to bestir ourselves, to give aid, to help out. As we mature, as we seriously take upon ourselves the teachings of the Buddha, we begin to see compassion as an actual responsibility, a duty, a virtuous attitude that must be made complete as part of our spiritual development. In the midst of limitless suffering in saṃsāra we should not wait to be moved; we should act with our own good resolve.

This divine abode has two advantages. First, it benefits us personally because it causes us to contemplate the central problem of our existence—dukkha, suffering—and it works against the inner defilements that keep us enmeshed in dukkha. The Buddha says, for example, that meditation on compassion results in the abandonment of cruelty. Have we ever been cruel? Does the ugly propensity to cruelty exist within us? We do not like to think of it, but it may be so. Hostile impulses and other bad habits left untouched do not vanish by themselves; they must be opposed and routed by counteracting powers; and for cruelty the antidote is compassion.

The second advantage to compassion is the benefit that follows for the world outside of us. A person who actively tries to arouse and practice compassion is the sort of person whom everybody hopes to meet in times of suffering. The world being full enough of violence, misfortune, illness, cruelty, deception, and menace of all kinds, everybody at one time or another needs sympathy, understanding, and effective aid. These the compassionate person is ready to give—and ready to give spontaneously, even without being asked.

Compassion is a beautiful inner quality that by its nature overflows the sphere of our immediate relations. To be virtuous followers of the Dhamma, we should certainly concern ourselves with the purification of our minds; but that purification proceeds by way of selfless acts toward the living beings we encounter. In the suffering of others we should recognize our own fragile and mortal condition, and we should be happy to prevent that suffering or relieve it where we can. We who hope for relief when we have done wrong or fallen into misery ought to realize that relief often depends on somebody's—even a stranger's—compassionate, selfless decision. Somebody, who doesn't have to, chooses to help us; and in that event we perceive—or should perceive—the bright exercise of virtue. That person performs a good action, good *kamma,* which serves simultaneously, without any conflict, for the welfare of both of us. We too have plenty of opportunities to think compassionately and act compassionately. How many, we must wonder, have we carelessly let pass?

Now, as the car bears us on without a pause, we might be thinking more or less definitely of how we could keep up sympathy and pity in ourselves. Looking out mindfully at the lives of others seems to do it, at least for a while—but are we just indulging in a sentimental sadness in the gray, lonely afternoon? How durable will our compassion prove, if it is really compassion that we feel? It seems we must work to achieve wholesome states. When this small trip ends, and we step out into the weather of our active life once again, how will we act?

The suffering of creatures being so pervasive, we might expect to get tired and turn away from gloom before very long. Who could keep commiserating all his hours? We have not, we fear, any saintly determination. And yet, we must remember that the Buddha speaks of two more divine abodes. Suffering is deep and terrible, but it is not only suffering on which we should fix our minds. Deep in this gigantic whirl of birth and death, there are still to be found laughter and bravery and good cheer. Many lovely deeds are done and many lovely results ensue. Shouldn't we give thought to those as well?

The third divine abode the Buddha speaks of is altruistic or appreciative joy. This is joy over the good fortune and good deeds of others, regardless of whether they are personally connected to us. It is a disinterested gladness at their gladness. Too often, engrossed in petty self-interest, we scarcely notice others' gladness, or we merely envy it without noticing what it tells us of the possibilities for happiness in this impermanent universe. Perhaps from time to time our own good luck or temporary satisfaction will cause us to look affably on others and approve of their happiness, but that is not much of a virtue. Here, as in so many other cases, the Buddha would have us act to arouse and maintain wholesome states—not just to wait around for a haphazard inspiration. It is possible to set about cultivating this altruistic joy, to make an effort to perceive goodness and brightness in the world, and to extend a hopeful, appreciative attitude toward living beings everywhere as they experience happiness as well as suffering.

As always, when we act according to Dhamma, benefits follow both for us and for the world. The Buddha says that when meditation on altruistic joy is developed, discontent is abandoned. Why should we assume that only good fortune happening for ourselves can give us pleasure or relieve our chronic discontent? We have all surely experienced at one time or another the swell of gladness in our hearts when we have admired without envy someone's luck and happiness. It may be that the question of *who* possesses the luck and happiness is of minor consequence. That living beings rejoice, that they do good, that they survive with grace the challenges before them—how excellent! how heartening! Wouldn't it be wise to devote ourselves more frequently to such an outlook?

The means for altruistic joy are available all the time, even in this afternoon of bleak skies and withered leaves. Look over there at the lonely land sweeping by, where the universe reveals its manifold nature once again. A man is painting the metal railing on his front porch. Concentrating on his work, he holds a can of paint in one hand and dabs delicately with a little brush. He doesn't have to do it; the railing would serve just as well unpainted; and nobody is going to stop and congratulate him; but he paints for the sake of neatness or beauty or some sense of order and dignity that he values. And amid the great collapse of autumn and the aging and crumbling of all things mortal, is this not a fair deed that he does? Does it not deserve our salutes and praises?

Over there on a hillside where laundry sways on a line, a woman playfully chases a tot, catches him up, giggling, and swings him in the air. Under the gray, grim heavens there are deaths and illnesses without number; there are quarrels and losses and troubles of all kinds; but there are flashes of joy, too. We fly on past all these scenes, gathering the perceptions we must use to figure out the world.

As we pass a crossroads far out in the country, two men jovially hail each other across the parking lot of a grocery. They laugh and gesture—in meeting or in parting, we cannot tell. Why do they laugh? Why do they smile so and shake their heads? The unsmiling universe does not require it. Does the pleasantry they share especially inspire them, or is it the simple working out of humanity and friendliness? We who are terrifically rushed down the highway will not know, but it does not matter. We are just pleased that they *do* smile, that they choose to gladden and be glad despite the heedless hurrying on of nature.

So various are the conditions of living beings that in contemplating them we could grow dizzy and bewildered, endlessly alternating between elation and sorrow, unless we try to rise toward the steadiness of the divine abodes. Those fair states do not consist in just an emotional surrender to scenes of pathos or of cheer. Loving kindness, compassion, and altruistic joy are virtuous attitudes that we ought to summon up intelligently, establish by our own calm will, and spread out as widely as we can. It does no good to fall sobbing and groaning over others' misery, or to gush insincerely over others' good fortune. The divine abodes are divine in that they remain unshaken, dignified, and serene in a universe that is mostly wild and desperate.

The fourth divine abode, in fact, is equanimity itself—a fine, free state of evenness and non-disturbance expanded outward over all the unevenness and disturbance that beings undergo. If we are practicing the Dhamma properly, we will wish that living beings may be free from misery, but whether they are or not we should try to lift up and fortify our own minds and look out over saṃsāra's roughness patiently and philosophically. In the ordinary upsets of our lives, we know very well that we appreciate those who show us personal benevolence and compassion, but we also appreciate, admire, and gratefully rely on those mature persons who remain calm amid both strife and good fortune. Their equanimity toward their own as well as others' interests gives us a sweet hint of higher worlds and nobler states of mind and heartens us to bear up under passing troubles.

Why should we not, observing equanimity in others and feeling its benign effects, determine to experience it and use it ourselves? The universe by its nature fluctuates, and we will never hold it and shape it to our satisfaction. Many ills and evils will go unchecked, and many blessings will dim and die away in spite of our desire, in spite of all our yearning or resentment. But the Buddha declares that when meditation on equanimity is developed, aversion is abandoned. Annoyance, enmity, and malice begin to weaken when equanimity spreads out pacifically over creatures. We live in saṃsāra, after all, where impermanence and destruction are normal. The landscape is varied, though, and full of fruitful mysteries, so should we not regard it mindfully just as it is, without infatuation and without anger?

Round about us in the rocking car the warmish breeze—maybe the very last gentleness of autumn—sweeps and swirls full of earthy scents. Yellow leaves fall out of the gray heavens and fly suddenly over the windshield and out of sight. Thinned-out woods run by us for a while then give way to flat stretches of farmland where work has ceased and only a few crows and doves are moving. Then once more we race past clusters of houses, where there are troubles we cannot mend and joys we cannot grasp, all multiplying outward beyond our imagination. Let us try to stay balanced and not admit needless affliction to our hearts. We observe that cat over there sitting on a lawn chair, peacefully licking a paw. It looks up calmly as we go by.

We cast a quiet look around the interior of the car, glancing at our friends who share this adventure. One is nodding off; another stares curiously at the landscape passing by. The driver pipes up with a funny anecdote, then abruptly falls silent. We note their quirks, remember their foibles, and remember too how genially they bear with our own peculiarities. Today we share a small experience—we are always sharing experiences, here on this human plane—so shouldn't we make ourselves more sympathetic travelers? Around us all the moist breeze slips and sighs, and around us all immemorial and unthinkable worlds revolve. We are all mortal, every one of us, mortal and aspiring, each in our dim and secret byways, toward some inexpressible realm of peace.

How weak our sympathy for beings still is, and how much it needs to grow. The Buddha explains how a noble disciple who has properly disciplined his mind and body goes on to regard the world at large:

Then, headman, that noble disciple—who is thus devoid of cov-
etousness, devoid of ill will, unconfused, clearly comprehending, ever
mindful—dwells pervading one quarter with a mind imbued with
loving kindness; likewise the second quarter, the third quarter, and
the fourth quarter.... He dwells pervading one quarter with a mind
imbued with compassion...with a mind imbued with altruistic
joy...with a mind imbued with equanimity; likewise the second
quarter, the third quarter, and the fourth quarter. Thus above,
below, across, and everywhere, and to all as to himself, he dwells per-
vading the entire world with a mind imbued with equanimity, vast,
exalted, measureless, without hostility, without ill will.

(Saṃyutta Nikāya 42:8)

These are grand ideals, to be sure, but they are ideals of action, not of luck. That is to say, whether or not benevolence is fortuitously bloom-ing within us, we can still act; we can still exert ourselves for the good. If right now we do not feel any expansive kindness toward all the world, that does not matter—let us just go ahead and try to generate wholesome thoughts. Here as everywhere in the teaching of the Buddha we find this inspiring principle, this confidence in the power of human action. We *can* rise to nobler states—and we should.

Our gaze is traveling among the russet oak trees on a distant ridge, and time seems grown immense and endless—when we notice that our car is slowing down. Now it turns off the highway down a small road, and turns again, and glides past a row of houses, and finally stops. The engine dies, and here we are, shoving open a creaking door and climbing out stiffly onto a newly quieted earth.

Now voices start up again, and everybody is stretching and milling around. Friends are coming down the walk to greet us. Over all of us and over the neighborhood a slow autumn breeze blows, cooler now, bear-ing here and there in the distance a few twirling leaves. The gray after-noon sky has lightened in one quarter. It seems a change is coming down from the north, and we may expect a deep, cold sky with stars when we drive back this evening. Then we shall look out again and guess at the sorrows in all the small, lit houses scattered out remotely on the earth.

But now there are friends before us, and other people we do not know—all of them mortal, all of them subject to cares—waiting to see what they shall receive from us in the way of fellowship. In all the four quarters of the changing world living beings wait thus, and above, below, across, and everywhere. Remembering them, straightening ourselves, stepping up with a fresh will, we approach these faces before us with a smile.

4. Alone Between Past and Future

When we seriously enter into a study of the teaching of the Buddha, we should quickly realize that progress toward the ending of suffering depends in good part on how well we perceive and understand what goes on around us moment by moment. It is not a matter of possessing a fabulous intellect or extraordinary senses but of paying attention as well as we can and noticing the internal and external signs that the world continually displays. By absorbing, considering, and pondering the Dhamma that the Buddha explains, we prepare ourselves to observe better. Observing dangers and opportunities as they occur in our own experience, we must then act honorably, in a timely and definite way, to restrain the unwholesome and increase the wholesome in our own minds.

But when we set ourselves to formal meditation, or simply to more disciplined observation in daily life, we may become bewildered by the speed and force of sights, sounds, smells, tastes, touch sensations, and mental objects. We may discover also that daydreaming, mental wandering, imagining, and vaguely straying are not just the foibles but rather the overriding habits of our minds. How often, indeed, do we really detect and contemplate a moment as it happens? Our life, it seems, is mainly reveries and speculations—lengthy forays into times gone by and times not come or never to be. We draw back from these at rare and unpredictable intervals; we emerge to find the clock ticking on the wall or to hear the doorbell ringing or to smell supper in the kitchen as sudden evidences of life's immediacy and transitoriness. Where have we been? Where are we now? We adjust briefly, getting out of our chairs, willing hands and feet to do their work—but too soon we get lost again in the cloudy landscapes of thought.

Mostly it is happenings outside of us that recall us to present business, not often a real initiative of mind. The drowsy flux of hopes and fancies goes on and on, distracting us from the present, the only free space in eternity where we can act and gain the good. We consider noble action as a possibility gone by or not yet attainable. Oh, *last* year, we reflect fondly, was a crazy time when we might have revolutionized our character and sought new truth—if only we had roused ourselves! And the future, just out of reach, fairly shines with tantalizing promise. Maybe *then* we shall at last begin to save our slippery hours from forgetfulness and become altogether better than we were. Maybe we shall—or maybe not.

We look up from dreams, and it is always the incomplete present, not yet come to fullness, not yet offering, we think, the exact right moment in which to act. Today, for example, we find this familiar body reposing in a soft chair and discover a book in our hands and mundane thoughts in our minds. Somewhere there is the hum of the refrigerator or the sighing of the furnace. There is a flickering of sunlight in the window. Truth has been flowing on and we have missed it.

Sounds of this flow have reached us throughout our weeks and years, as have swirling colors, smells, flavors, touch sensations, and fascinating thoughts. Plenty of these have appeared to make use of. Plenty of the material of existence pours through us daily; but real and rich as it may be, it drowns us strangely in abstraction; it leaves us always gazing elsewhere, dreaming, remote from the present moment. We miss again and again the true nature of things that is manifest before our senses, and because we miss, because we fail to pay attention, we flounder on drearily in seas of doubt and sadness, never coming to land.

What can we do? Ignorant desire will rule us if reason cannot. Aggrieved by the incompleteness of the present, we yearn for the past; we revise it in imagination, then remember it is gone and grow sadder. Or we aspire toward the future; we conceive of fresh joys, dread new pains, and realize at last, dolefully, that it is still today in which we suffer. Perhaps in the rare moments when a chance sight or sound brings us to brief balance, we begin to wonder whether it is possible to walk deliberately and with equanimity in the present, comprehending all the flashes of life as they happen, but every time we tentatively determine to observe and learn, some new current of distraction leads us off.

It is strange and dispiriting that all this flood of sensation should conduct us not to a better knowledge of reality but only to more reveries, speculations, and weary misgivings. We are avid to understand ourselves and interested in the minute twinges of our emotions, but the more we try to resolve the mysteries of our subjective experience, the farther we stray from the present moment and thus from life. Again and again we scramble back in embarrassment, dully aware that more minutes, or whole hours or days, have drained away and left no wisdom behind. How is it that we fail to be peaceful in the present?

From a Buddhist point of view, the past appears as former states of being that we ought to learn from but not attempt to recover, for there is no refuge there; and the future appears only as possibilities to prepare for sensibly—in the practical way of saving money or fixing the roof before the rain comes—but otherwise not worried about, for the present moment is the only arena for action. Such a view, if it went no further than this, might not seem remarkable. Surely we would like to live untroubled in the present, but we cannot or do not. What then can Buddhism say to us?

First of all, we need to understand that all we have to work with are our actions expressed by way of body, speech, and mind. These occur in the present; thus attention to the present is vital. Once done, once launched into the world, actions will have their good or bad effects and are not subject to revision or recall. It is certainly wise to remember those actions and to identify our mistakes and our good choices, but to dwell upon them, to gruelingly to rake over, relive, or reform each blurry minute of memory, is both painful and futile. We exhaust ourselves, and the actual, breathing moment we live in is not improved. Similarly, the Buddha teaches us not to become absorbed in speculations about the future. The future will not come to be through our choices alone but also through innumerable and inconceivably complex other conditions. It is not that we should take no interest in the future, but rather that we should prepare for the future by wisely attending to matters immediately at hand; that is, by acting with kindness, honor, diligence, and self-control here and now, knowing that whatever circumstances will come upon us in the future will carry the impression of our present deeds.

Furthermore, the Buddha gives us a means of preventing our attention from wandering from the vital present and of discovering what is important within it. It is not enough (as we have perhaps already discovered) to agree theoretically that an attitude of coolness or equanimity toward past and future is sensible and healthy and that we should stay attentive to the present. For all our philosophizing, we are subject to great winds of passion, and our little edifice of reason is quickly toppled unless we build it from well-observed experience as well as from written and spoken doctrine. The Buddha advises us to observe and to discipline our senses in such a way that we do not become overwhelmed by the objects of perception, but remain able to consider them independently for what they are. It is not that the minute details of an object, or its overall appearance, are necessarily significant. Rather what is required for a fruitful understanding of anything is the way we approach it and the way we conduct ourselves toward it.

Specifically, the Buddha says that the well-taught noble disciple "regards what is seen, heard, sensed, cognized, attained, sought after, ranged over by the mind thus: 'This is not mine; this I am not; this is not myself'" (*Majjhima Nikāya* 22:16). Both what we think of as the world at large and the material form, feeling, perception, mental formations, and consciousness that constitute our personality should be considered in this way. All objects of perception and the organs of perception themselves should be treated with this same cool recollection because, first of all, it acknowledges truth, and, second, because it helps us to stay balanced in the present and understand it without distortion from any partiality.

Whatever aspect of reality, whatever idea or perception or material thing that we consider as our self or as belonging to our self turns out to be, when we examine it, always impermanent, transitory, unreliable, and hence empty of those stable qualities we would like to impute to it. Instead of regarding things as "mine" in any absolute, egoistic sense or trying to find the mysterious center of our being in this or that phenomenon, we should try to get rid of the great, obfuscating cloud of what the Buddha calls the "I am" conceit. This can be done by frequently remembering and reflecting that what are here in these various sensory perceptions are ultimately only impermanent, passing phenomena, not parts of a self or ego.

When we unconsciously assume an attitude of identification or ownership toward the sights, sounds, smells, tastes, touches, and mental phenomena that race through our sense organs, we have already begun to misperceive them—for they actually cannot be held still and possessed and preserved. No matter how energetic our reasoning may be, we are only working with shadows and phantoms and cannot attain any real peace. Vainly conceiving them as "mine," we are led to dead ends in thought again and again, because all objects that we turn to with this attitude change and disappear—hence the long, exhausting groping into past and future.

It is certainly necessary to think, to ponder the Dhamma, to reason on the basis of sound principles; but it is not necessary to adore or to chase after every flutter of "my" imagination, emotion, opinion, or mood. Rather we should employ the Buddha's cautionary reflection, remembering that any phenomenon that has arisen is fundamentally not "mine" or self at all—it is just a conditioned thing that by nature arises and passes away. If this attitude is well established, much useless infatuation will be forestalled, and we will be prepared to investigate in an unbiased way.

Such investigation, together with careful reflection on Buddhist doctrine, yields informative experience that inspires virtuous action by speech and body. Never will we just think our way to happiness, never reason suffering out of existence, never pretend our way to peace. If we review the problems that assail us—the doubts, conflicts, and regrets—with an attitude of clinging, not considering that they are really not ours nor parts of our self, we can easily slump into a brooding introspection that neglects the world and gives us nothing but more unhappy states of mind. We may hope we are figuring out answers, contemplating solutions; but mostly we go on chewing juiceless stalks, crunching the chaff of thought and getting no nourishment. This is not correct meditation. To meditate is not to ruminate strenuously on our problems, not to shut off the world in order to indulge at length our private feelings, but rather to draw back a little way from internal as well as external phenomena so as to see them all more disinterestedly and hence more clearly.

All of us are concerned chiefly with our own happiness, and we instinctively suppose (without good instruction to the contrary) that what we need is a fine examination of all our subjective wants, and then precise and abundant satisfactions. But genuine happiness is to be found rather in detached, disinterested contemplation of the sensations that pass through the mind, without attempts to grasp them or pretend ownership of them. Happiness visits us in those moments when we maintain a neutral, unexcited view and act according to noble principles. We cannot by any purely intellectual or emotional efforts establish peace in our minds while we continue to bear down exclusively on subjective pain or pleasure in the belief that understanding and relief are only possible within the palpitating limits of our personality. Contrary to this powerful instinct, the Buddha teaches us to cease clinging and to look heedfully at the world—that is, at the panorama of sense-phenomena—and to remember that none of it is ultimately "me" or anything belonging to "me."

This perspective marvelously sets free our strength. Instead of straining miserably and futilely to arrest the change in things we like, we should stand back a little, giving up vain claims and presumptions (which nature in any case ignores), and look on life from a cooler distance. Then, not carried off to dreams of past or future, we may see where we can profitably apply our powers.

The reflection, "This is not mine; this I am not; this is not myself" is the full, conscious expression of a principle that we may have been unaware of but that has probably influenced us for the good already: that we become freer and less troubled to the degree that we look upon things in the world without a sense of possession and prerogative. For example, in early childhood we become aware that there are other beings in the world who are *not us*—who are entirely distinct and sufficient to themselves—and this understanding eventually teaches us to adapt, to one degree or another, to the inevitable demands and dangers of life. We realize that if we are to enjoy peace and harmony we must respect other beings and their interests, and we must acknowledge limits to our reach. Indeed, how well we absorb the lesson that *we* do not dominate reality is a good measure of our maturity as conscious beings.

As we grow up we learn—or should learn—that to restrain the surges of conceit within us is to rise in the estimation of our friends and colleagues. When we study and practice the Dhamma, moreover, we should learn that to observe from a standpoint of ego in any degree is to observe imperfectly, and that an unbiased, disinterested view is one that will yield the most useful knowledge. Right mindfulness show us things from different angles, just as they really exist; it takes no sides—it just reveals the wholesome and the unwholesome and the indifferent in their naked states. Then, when the Dhamma we have heard as doctrine becomes manifest in experience, we gain faith that the principles of behavior that the Buddha urges upon us really do work for our welfare. As we learn to subordinate our inborn, heedless desires to these honorable principles, we are relieved of much frustration and enabled to use our strength for (it is to be hoped) higher and nobler purposes.

Understanding the value of the passing moment, we ought to treat it with more care as a source of knowledge and as an opportunity for actions that will develop into the future. If we skip over the present in our hunger for the past or the future or the wholly imaginary, we will acquire no useful knowledge from the crowding signals of our senses and will miss the chance to store up wholesome deeds. In the meantime we will still be generating kamma—intentional action—but arbitrarily and without judgment. If we remain mindful and collected, however, we can both learn and act astutely.

Let us consider what states of mind we wish to have right now and what we hope will mature in the future. If we wish to entertain what is morally good and uplifting and to see it growing healthily, we should restrain the impulse to grasp and try to perceive freshly and without bias what is happening now around us and within us, whether that is agreeable or disagreeable. Clear perception is not a matter of giving our attention exclusively to pleasant, appealing, or beautiful things, but rather of observing calmly whatever is actually occurring. We should take note of the causes and conditions that bring about and maintain our present states of mind, be they depressing or gladdening; then, remembering the teaching of the Buddha, we should exert ourselves to expel the bad and build up the good. Thus the slippery moment, whatever its tone or flavor, does not uselessly pass away but gives us real benefit. Working intently for the good is itself a present blessing.

To live conscientiously in the present does not require superhuman concentration—just a steady application of mindfulness, a conscious acknowledgment simply of what is happening. This need not be anything striking or unusual. We have only to look around, or to pause and remember where we are, to find convenient objects in the present. For example, we may be sitting in a chair and turning the page of a book, feeling our fingers sliding down the edge of the paper. Let us just know the moment, register it, acknowledge it without any special cogitation. Or we are walking down the sidewalk with cold rain blowing against us. Let us know that, too, acknowledging the present facts of rain, wind, and cold. Or we are standing in an office, turning and lifting books and papers and noticing sounds echoing about us. In another moment we are in the kitchen of our house, shutting the door of a cabinet with an easy push, noticing the faint pressure on our fingertips. Then we are standing at a window and watching the sunset, or methodically dabbing toothpaste on a brush, or speaking, sitting, or standing in one way or another. All this is the rich and subtle present, to be learned from with mindfulness.

It is not that one superlative moment within the flood of sensory experience will erupt with spectacular and unique truth. All phenomena, the boring and the thrilling alike, exhibit the same characteristics of impermanence, unsatisfactoriness, and nonself; and the purpose of mindfulness directed toward the passing moment is to comprehend not just the particular but also the universal—the operation everywhere of the same tremendous principle of conditionality. When, with time and diligence, we perceive that all things in the world are brought about by conditions, and cease with the subsiding of those conditions, we become more aware of the wretchedness of vanity—for our own momentary personality is also a conditioned thing that must change. When we perceive that our actions leave their marks on us and bring results, we realize we should undertake what is good and resist what is bad. When we perceive with mindfulness the disappearance of what is dear and precious to us, we are schooled in the wisdom of nongrasping. Gradually the Buddha's words, planted in the soil of our minds and watered by experience, give rise to fresh growth.

Today, it may be, we sit alone for a while, trying to perceive the growth of wholesome states within; and indeed such periods of solitude can help judicious contemplation. But insight into the laws of existence does not occur just from settling down in a comfortable environment, or from grinding away doggedly on speculations about the past or the future. Solitude may give us room to contemplate at length; but if we are careless and unprepared, it may only excite more inner chatter. Whether we have temporarily retired from society or are making our way in the midst of commotion, we still must find a profounder solitude and independence by giving up familiar and nearly automatic assumptions about what does or should belong to us.

In the Pāli Canon there is a mention of an eccentric, solitary monk who goes about his business quite alone, who walks alone, sits alone, and meditates alone, and who praises dwelling alone. To him the Buddha says this:

> That is a way of dwelling alone, Elder, I do not deny this. But as to how dwelling alone is fulfilled in detail, listen to that and attend closely; I will speak.... Here, Elder, what lies in the past has been abandoned, what lies in the future has been relinquished, and desire and lust for present forms of individual existence have been thoroughly removed. It is in such a way, Elder, that dwelling alone is fulfilled in detail.
>
> (Saṃyutta Nikāya 21:10)

It is not necessarily physical solitude that the Buddha recommends, but rather the profounder solitude—or the radical independence—of living aloof from attachment to the vanished past, the inchoate future, and even the shifting forms of our experience in the present moment. We should not forget the past; nor should we fail to consider the future we are daily preparing through our many actions; but we should renounce all vain interest in grasping after anything in those inaccessible realms. By such renunciation our attention, which otherwise might roam forever, lost and sickly and diffuse, is brought down to the present, to this one spot in eternity that matters, this one field for meaningful action.

Here in the present the Buddha would have us thoroughly remove "desire and lust for present forms of individual existence." What can this mean? If anything is dear to us, it is this conviction of an individual existence that we imagine in some way belongs to us. We can, perhaps, conceive of a solitude of independence from past and future, wherein we are only concerned, in mindful, bright economy, with our business in the present moment. But how could we possibly abandon more?

These present forms of individual existence—these formations, patterns of aggregates, panoramas of sense experience—are only *present* forms, not eternal substances, and since the present moment is always passing away, when we indulge in desire and lust for any of its aspects we are craving more phantoms like the phantoms of the past and the future. Thus even in the trembling instant when we think we are attending to what is real, we can still get lost in vast realms of abstraction. To appreciate, to value the present moment does not mean to treat it as any more secure than any other segment of time, or to pounce on momentary profits and pleasures, or to become enamored of whatever is novel and gaudy and trifling. Even our own life—these present, flashing forms of thought and experience—is a matter of changing conditions that should be regarded without desire and lust just as changing conditions.

What is valuable about this moment is not that it is new, novel, and *now* (because it is still, like all moments, transient and unsubstantial) but rather that it offers us the chance to perceive directly the arising and passing away of phenomena and to act, to produce wholesome kamma, and thereby to launch fresh goodness into the world.

When desire and lust are removed, the world does not vanish, but delusion about it vanishes. Would it not be good to be free from delusion?

When we sleep, let us sleep, but when we wake—as now, mindfully turning the page of a book in this day in this universe—there is the work of the wakeful to accomplish.

5. *The Ritual Element*

BOOKS WILL GO A LONG WAY toward satisfying our wish to understand the teaching of the Buddha, but most of us sooner or later feel the need to establish contact with Buddhism as it exists as a living institution. For one thing, we are curious about how those who have called themselves Buddhists for a long time conduct their ceremonies and what sort of communal fellowship they maintain. For another, we are probably looking, very tentatively, for some sort of spiritual friendship ourselves and would like to get a feel for the atmosphere in monasteries or temples where Buddhists congregate.

Suppose, then, we manage to make a visit to a Theravāda Buddhist temple on the occasion of some regular observance or special ceremony. More than likely we find ourselves sitting at the back of a shrine room, uncomfortably shifting on the carpet and craning our necks to see over the people in front of us to the monks, who are chanting or bowing or doing something incomprehensible with incense and candles. Other people appear to know what is happening, but we visitors do not. The monks chant in Pāli, we know, but even if books with translations are within reach, we are too distracted to find the place, too busy looking around at the furnishings of the room, or too embarrassed to ask for explanations. Some kind of ceremony is under way—not a very elaborate one, as far as we can tell—and although at first we are mildly interested in the proceedings we find that we get tired pretty quickly and begin to wonder what this can possibly have to do with the austere regimen of meditation we have come to think of as Buddhism.

A visit to any traditional Asian Buddhist temple, or even a casual leafing through photographs of Buddhist ceremonies, will certainly arouse a great many questions and quite possibly much mystification, because Buddhism as it is lived and practiced traditionally appears quite different from the largely intellectual discipline that might have attracted us in the first place. Why should anyone bother with chanting, bowing, offering food to monks, and all the rest? How is it that, after a good deal of reading, we still know so little of these rituals and devotions? Have we, in being so intent on philosophy and meditation technique, possibly overlooked important matters of social life?

A study of books can provide us with a preliminary or even quite advanced technical knowledge of Buddhist doctrine. If we exercise our memories well we can acquire a pretty good grasp of the principal tenets, enough to let us see that here is a majestic system built on reason and keenly observed experience that appears to lead (if we are willing to follow it) to emancipation from suffering. But after a time even the best of books leaves us reaching vaguely toward something we cannot touch, groping for palpable experience to connect with all this deep, engrossing thought. We might go on for quite a while, even indefinitely, contemplating the Dhamma wistfully as a private, wholly mental thing, without seeing how it could ever enter our lives in a definite, unashamedly religious sense. We esteem the teaching but cannot seem to make it thrive in the secular atmosphere of work, shopping center, and home. Here in the books, we realize, are ideas of great beauty. How can we get fruit from them? How can we pass from intellectual interest to practiced faith?

For most of us born in the Western world, remote from Buddhism of any institutional kind, knowledge of the Dhamma has come entirely from books and, occasionally, spoken words, some quite excellent and informative, certainly. But this kind of learning still retains a somewhat ethereal air in the absence of actions, traditions, and spiritual observances in which we can participate. That the Buddhist religion has survived so long in the world is a result not so much of the durability of manuscripts as of the power of ideas embodied in custom; and custom, for all our abundant sources of information, is what we lack and cannot in the long run do without. Books crumble easily enough; thought crumbles faster, if not made firm by some sort of concrete practice that holds together believers and sees to the transmission of the teaching to the young.

The modern world with its quickly accessible pleasures, its entertainments, hobbies, and intellectual pastimes, inclines us to suppose that religion, too, can be selected piecemeal, can be appreciated, assembled, and indulged in precisely to the degree and in the manner that we prefer. We like to read about enlightenment; we like to meditate a little, when it suits us. We may even like to exercise our minds by studying some of the profound philosophical discourses of the Buddha. Nowadays it is not hard to satisfy ourselves at least with respect to these limited, namable interests. Having read books, attended lectures, practiced meditation, admired Buddhist art, and chatted amiably with other seekers, we have done pretty much all we had in mind to do. And yet, disconcertingly, we are not enlightened; we are not even confident of moving in the direction of enlightenment. Even if we are inspired by our studies, we remain in some sense perplexingly alone, outside the grand, historical flow of the Dhamma, waiting disconsolately for spiritual fulfillment as an entirely private blessing.

Why should this be so? If we have investigated everything we like, should we not be satisfied in a deeper sense than we are? But perhaps we have passed a little too blithely over important matters. One thing that contemporary society especially fosters is the assumption that each individual intuitively knows or can confidently decide what is useful in tradition and what is not. So we read and we reject; or we read and approve with qualifications, briskly skipping through the lines of ancient teaching; or perhaps we read and enthusiastically accept everything, taking it all as understood even if it is not. For most of our lives society around us has been offering us things, urging activities upon us, suggesting countless measures for recreation, education, and employment, so even with regard to handed-down Buddhist teaching, we feel quite disposed to edit, abbreviate, and rearrange according to our pleasure. If, then, the fragments we finally approve of do not over time sustain us spiritually, we grow skeptical and gloomy, thinking we have done what should be necessary, selected and revised as is our unquestionable right, and yet found the effects wanting. Should we now fault the teaching? Or should we revisit some unexamined assumptions?

When we study a doctrine that is new to us (although it might be very old) and find in it points that coincide with our private opinions and theories, we are naturally cheered—and certainly we could never adopt any doctrine if it did not at least partly correspond to our own deeply pondered intuitions. This, without doubt, is natural and reasonable. But to go on to decide that a certain teaching is worthwhile simply because it echoes our established opinion is very unwise. Along that easy course there is no new discovery of truth, only more stale habit.

Similarly, when we read of teachings contrary to our preferences and outside the realm of our usual consideration, we tend to reject them automatically. They are strange and intellectually disturbing—hence they must be wrong. This tendency, too, is quite natural; and certainly our native intelligence and worldly experience should alert us to what is outlandish and incoherent. But it is good to remember that a new or an old way of considering and dealing with life is not false just because it surprises us or contradicts our theories. A sincere seeker should compare ideas for the purpose of gaining a closer fix on truth.

When investigating Buddhism, then, we ought to give some thought to the cultural and intellectual background out of which we peer. Are we indeed entirely qualified to decide what is meaningful in the tradition and what is not? And why should we suppose that this present age—which is not without its cruelties and contradictions—naturally stands above all others in moral insight and affords us a superior view? We have perhaps assumed a little too quickly that we can (as we do in so many other fields) select exactly what we like and then declare it comprehensive and true.

Sadly, contemporary tastes, to which we might at least in part conform, seem to run counter to major parts of the teaching of the Buddha. The essential doctrine of rebirth, for example, may strike us as strange and fantastic, even frightening, and thus not to be considered at all or else to be relegated to the category of quaint, outmoded beliefs to smile at and pass over. That there should actually be heavenly worlds and hellish worlds and beings born in them likewise seems unmodern and thus dubious and negligible. The moral teachings of the Buddha, too—those warnings about the dangers in killing, stealing, sexual misconduct, lying, and other sorts of misbehavior—seem a little too restrictive in areas where we have come to prefer ample latitude; so we might prefer to take them in a more figurative sense and apply them, if at all, with our presumably nimble, contemporary intelligence. Then too, in a secular age, the ritual or devotional aspects of Buddhism may seem out of place. Perhaps (we suppose) they satisfied the wants of ancient, unedified ages, but they could hardly do for us today, whom the idea of formal humility makes strangely uncomfortable.

It is this last aspect of Buddhism—the ritual element—that is perhaps most often misunderstood, rejected, or just left out of consideration by students in the West but that might after all be the link to the fuller spiritual life that seems so elusive. If we were to suspend our prerogative to decide in a minute what is good in twenty-five centuries of Buddhism, we might get a better view of how the parts of the tradition have functioned together for so long and might even discover some pleasant and useful features.

What exactly do we mean by ritual? We speak the phrase "rites and rituals," usually with a tinge of disapproval or contempt, to refer to gestures, ceremonies, and other religious formalities that we suppose are carried out in lieu of genuine spiritual experience and are therefore pointless. But are all such activities necessarily pointless? Do we really understand what is involved in particular ceremonies or, beyond that, what vital insights of the Buddha might underlie them?

To clear up this matter we must go back, as in so many important cases, to the Buddha himself, whose attitude toward rites, rituals, vows, ceremonies, ascetic observances, and the like was neither categorically favorable nor categorically dismissive but instead calmly pragmatic. Understanding that a noble, contented life and freedom from suffering come about from distinct conditions, the Buddha taught his followers to gather and build up those conditions in their daily lives. To the extent that rituals or devotional practices provide such good conditions they are worth performing. What we have to do, then, is to pay attention to the effects of such practices on our own minds. If they promote understanding, calm, contentment, and an attitude of forbearance and kindness toward living beings, they may be useful; if they arouse confusion, anger, conceit, or other defilements, they are harmful and not to be pursued.

One of the "fetters" *(saṃyojanas)* that keep us bound to the cycle of suffering is "grasping after rules and observances" *(sīlabbataparāmāsa)*. This is the tendency to cling to ascetic practices, rituals, rules, procedures, and other special formalities as a means of attaining enlightenment or ensuring worldly prosperity. Simply going through the motions of any religious custom is not beneficial, as it may easily substitute for and entirely crowd out the vital, inner cultivation of virtue, concentration, and wisdom—thus keeping the practitioner, no matter how punctilious, still revolving through the sorrows of birth and death. Such thoughtless ritualizing is aesthetically attractive; it is easy (in that the exertions involved are mechanical and intellectually undemanding and do not require any change in overall behavior); and it gives a vague sense of accomplishing *something*—but it fetters the unwary ever more tightly to the realm of suffering.

It is not the observances themselves that are necessarily harmful but rather the tendency—indeed, the common human compulsion—to grasp at them and invest them with imaginary power. The Buddha certainly had no dislike of structure, discipline, and decorum; he himself was a careful maker and expounder of rules for the Sangha of monks and nuns. He established many principles, standards, and procedures for his ordained disciples to observe, both in moral discipline and in workaday, communal business, so that an environment favorable to the wholesome development of the mind could be maintained. There being a strong relationship between external comportment and inner development, good rules and dignified customs are certainly worth respecting— they just cannot be expected to bring enlightenment by themselves.

The Buddha did not attempt to introduce religious rituals for his lay followers. He had, it would seem, no interest in upsetting the etiquette and the harmless traditions of the society of his time, as he was intent on the far more vital matter of teaching a way of wise and virtuous behavior that would lead people out of the morass of suffering. He did, however, speak against the cruel practice of killing animals in sacrifices; and he prohibited the monks from getting their living by practicing low arts like magic and fortune-telling.

The first lay people who listened to the Buddha and gained faith in the Dhamma did not take on any special new system of rites and ceremonies. Rather, in a natural, unforced way, they adapted their ancestral customs to accommodate the few needs of the monastic community, the Sangha; and the Buddha directed the Sangha, as it grew, so it would not become an unwelcome burden upon the laity but would remain an inspiration and a guide. The ceremonies in which the laity participated developed over the centuries according to what was convenient and agreeable in the various lands and cultures to which the Dhamma spread.

For Buddhists today, as in ancient times, particular ceremonies or rituals might be good or bad, depending on the motivations behind them and their consequent effects; but clinging or grasping, as the Buddha saw, is always bad. It involves a resignation of intelligence and leads to an excess of externals—ever more elaborate rituals in which symbols are exhausted by repetition and the essential Dhamma is obscured by formalities originally meant to point to it. Regardless of the intensity of one's hope, no zealous performance of ritual will accomplish that which must be accomplished through the direct, daily cultivation of virtue, concentration, and wisdom. The follower of the good Dhamma is expected to live according to the "middle way"—that is to say, moderately and judiciously—using traditions wisely and following precepts conscientiously out of a calm understanding of the good acts they may inspire.

Making vows, aspirations, and resolutions is, like performing prescribed rites, a kind of traditional, ritual practice that may be helpful or useless, depending on our underlying attitudes and the kind of behavior they promote. Here, too, a purely mechanical observance obscures what is indispensable for our spiritual advancement: our intentional actions of refraining from the bad and cultivating the good. If we formally resolve, for example, to discipline ourselves more seriously in meditation or to strive harder in daily life to overcome defilements, that is fine as far as it goes; but in itself it does not signify very much. Let us see what good deeds will follow our ritual pronouncements.

The Buddha gives an amusing simile to illustrate the uselessness of aspirations without accompanying wise actions:

> *Suppose a man needing oil, seeking oil, wandering in search of oil were to heap up gravel in a tub, sprinkle it all over with water, and press it. Then, if he made an aspiration...he would be unable to procure any oil; If he made no aspiration...he would be unable to procure any oil; if he both made an aspiration and made no aspiration...he would be unable to procure any oil; if he neither made an aspiration nor made no aspiration...he would be unable to procure any oil. Why is that? Because that is not a proper method for procuring oil.*
> (Majjhima Nikāya 126:10)

The proper method, the wise procedure, is crucial, not the wish in the mind. The Buddha goes on to say that if a man were to heap up sesame flour and press that, then regardless of whether he made an aspiration to procure oil, or made no aspiration, or *both* made and did not make an aspiration (perhaps wishing intermittently or half-heartedly), or *neither* made nor did not make an aspiration (perhaps trying to keep rigid neutrality in the matter), he would still be able to procure oil. It is just a fact of nature that oil appears when the sesame is pressed, and whatever aspirations, promises, or vows one makes toward that end are entirely secondary.

It is the same in the case of spiritual accomplishment. The Buddha says that if ascetics and brahmins hope to achieve some fruit from their holy life—their celibate, monastic discipline—and if they do in fact possess the factors of the Noble Eightfold Path—right view, right intention, right speech, right action, right livelihood, right effort, right mindfulness, right concentration—then they will be able to procure that fruit, irrespective of any aspirations, vows, or promises they make or do not make in the matter. If, on the other hand, they have *wrong* view, *wrong* intention, *wrong* speech, and so on, they will remain unable to procure any fruit from the holy life, regardless of their aspirations or lack of aspirations. Here as everywhere the law of causality underlies the fortune of living beings.

For lay people following the teaching of the Buddha nowadays, the principle is exactly the same: we must learn what are the necessary conditions for happiness and spiritual progress (in brief, the factors of the Noble Eightfold Path) and then see about putting together those conditions in a practical, reasonable way. If we want to participate in rituals, vows, and formal aspirations as a way of calming our minds or arousing enthusiasm and determination, there is no harm—there may indeed be benefit—as long as such practices are consonant with the Buddha's teaching and as long as we do not neglect the day-to-day requirements of a noble life.

For monks or nuns or lay people who are especially zealous and who incline toward asceticism, toward more rigorous efforts in mental development, the same principle applies. Any kind of ritual or meditation that we test should be evaluated according to the kinds of effects it produces in the mind, quite apart from how impressive it seems to others or to ourselves. The outer formalities of meditation—how exactly we sit or walk and how we incorporate chanting, bowing, or other religious customs—as well as the internal exercises in concentration and mindfulness, should always serve the end of mental purification. It is in fact hard to distinguish meditation from formalities or ceremony in the largest sense, because serious efforts to arouse mindfulness or dispel defilements or develop virtues naturally tend to occur in what we might call a ritual or ceremonial way, according to a dignified pattern. Thus, whether we are reciting Pāli verses or bowing or memorizing doctrine or carrying out some kind of meditative discipline, we should notice the patterns we engage in and observe their effects, not relying only on special words, gestures, and postures to bring about blessings. Rituals can help us or obstruct us, not according to their difficulty or perceived asceticism but according to the quality of the mental states they arouse.

Asked about the usefulness of ascetic practices and observances, the Buddha says that if, in carrying them out, unwholesome states grow and wholesome states decline, then those practices should not be carried out, but if wholesome states grow and unwholesome states decline, then those practices should indeed be carried out.

This pragmatic attitude is the best one to take, not just toward strict asceticism or self-discipline but toward all ceremonies, rites, rituals, and meditation techniques that may appeal to us. If they increase understanding of the Dhamma and if they stimulate faith, kindly thoughts, and determination to do what is virtuous, they are useful. If they arouse unwholesome mental states, such as fear, greed, conceit, anger, or confusion, they should be left alone.

Even if we do not like what we know of religious rituals and suppose all such formal practices useless, we ought to consider that even the most secular-minded person lives according to ritual of a sort and indeed cannot be happy without it. For what is ritual but a formal, accustomed, and graceful way of doing things? Chaos excites us but does not please us long; soon it exhausts and terrifies. We might live informally for the most part, dodging through the rough surprises of our days, but we like to come home to steadiness, to be able to hang our coat on the same worn hook, to sit down at the family dinner table according to satisfying custom, to put our children to bed with words and motions made dear by use and love. And over the years we find ourselves, as a matter of courtesy or instinct, observing many conventions among our friends and colleagues, many formalities and solemnities during which we slow down and try to act with at least a degree of dignity. Many occasions require it; and our hearts are such that we need to find meaning and weight in these moments of grief or joy or congratulation or condolence. These practices afford us a little peace and order amid the agitation of saṃsāra and help us to feel related to our ancestors and all others who have undergone the same human experiences. Domestic ease, social harmony, and steadfastness in the bitter crises of life all benefit from the reassurance of ritual.

While we sit on the carpet as visitors to a Theravāda temple we may or may not find the rituals we observe interesting at first look; but a knowledge not only of the purpose of specific actions but also of the beautiful philosophy beneath them might lead us gradually to appreciate and approve of some of these rituals. What, let us ask ourselves, are admirable human qualities that we would wish to see more often in the world around us? Faith, morality, humility, generosity, and reverence for the good come quickly to mind—and these are exactly the qualities that the best ceremonies promote.

Theravāda Buddhists customarily recite, in their own languages or in the ancient cadences of Pāli, a brief homage to the Buddha, the great teacher. Repeating line by line the stately phrases spoken by a monk, they announce that they go for refuge to the Buddha, to the Dhamma, and to the Sangha. They announce their resolution to abide by the five great precepts—to refrain from killing, stealing, sexual misconduct, lying, and taking intoxicants. They may formally request blessings or teachings from the monks, and the monks may chant discourses of the Buddha or other verses appropriate for the occasion. There may be bowing and lighting of candles and incense and placing of flowers and ringing of bells—these being symbols of reverence and comforting gestures that help the participants to feel the inspiring depth of Buddhist history and the flow of truth through generations.

There may be a formal talk, too, a sermon on some aspect of the Dhamma, bringing again to the listeners' minds those noble principles discovered long ago that remain still fresh today. At the time for the monks' main meal of the day, there will be a formal offering of food and a chanting of blessings by the assembled Sangha. The lay people offer what is most basic and most powerfully symbolic—food that renews strength, food that keeps the Sangha alive to preserve and pass on the precious Dhamma—and the Sangha responds by congratulating the givers on their virtuous deeds and wishing them long life, beauty, happiness, and strength.

All these deeds are "rites and rituals." Should we reject them? If we acknowledge the Buddha as our great teacher who out of compassion has shown the way to escape the wilderness of suffering, is it not fitting to speak a few words in his praise? Would it not be right and sensible and wise to seek refuge from life's perils in what is noble and pure—in the Buddha himself, in the majestic Dhamma he discovered, and in the Sangha, the community of noble disciples throughout the ages? Would it not be meritorious to offer food, in ritual and in practical generosity, to the monks and nuns who try to fulfill the discipline of the Buddha? Since the world everywhere has ills and temptations, and our minds are assailed by anger and greed, would it not do us good to take up the precepts of virtue and repeat them again and again so that we shall remember them and heed them honorably all our lives?

There is no need for Buddhists in the West to adopt all the rituals and usages of the East. Much of what we see in Asian Buddhist temples has grown up in and been shaped by cultural circumstances that are lacking in the West. Here we live in a different complex of language, history, and social convention, so it is entirely natural and suitable that the ritual element of Western Buddhism should develop differently in some respects, even as the monastic rules and the essential Dhamma are passed on reverently and, it is to be hoped, in unbroken purity.

At the same time, it would be unwise to spurn all handed-down ritual tradition and suppose that our unconsidered *likes* must be our only guides and that we can successfully patch together an entirely new and satisfactory system of observances. That way leads deeper into loneliness. Some old rituals have lasted so long and spread through so many lands because they beautifully embody universal human responses to the good Dhamma; so it would be well for us to contemplate them without haste, to read about them and consider, and to sit on the carpet in temples and observe for a little longer than discomfort or impatience would usually allow. Let us inform ourselves about what exactly is happening and what it is intended to represent, so that over time, as we try to make for ourselves a spiritual home in Buddhism, we will know what others have found good to use for walls and beams and graceful furnishings.

All good ritual connects the lonely, individual person to the greater community of those who have believed and strived throughout history. It assuages our sense of isolation and gives us, for a time at least, some significance amid the impermanence of nature. It focuses our will on the flickering, living moment wherein wisdom and peace are to be found.

6. Multiflora Rose

ON THIS UNUSUALLY HOT AFTERNOON in May we find ourselves out in the country, turning away from buildings and people to seek a little restorative solitude. Too much noise, too much crowding, too much argument have worn us out, and we believe from good experience that an hour or two traipsing through fields and woods will refresh us. How this happens, we have no idea, but it surely does, and even if we get no distinct inspirations as to how to solve our problems, that is all right—a brief calm is still welcome. Hawks are sailing far above us today like emblems of a fine detachment that we might achieve, and we are eager to be moving as well as we can.

So shall we cross this sweet-smelling, overgrown field here and duck into the woods beyond to escape the heat of the afternoon and the worse heat of thought? What absurdly cogitating creatures we are! The clash of wills and words we endure in company is apparently not enough for us—we go on overworking our minds to near exhaustion without anybody's provocation. So we had best start hiking at once and turn to the body's business. The brambles in our way at least have a nice factuality about them that we can deal with. Oh no, caught again! The thorns have got us. Let us take our time here and gently unhook ourselves. It is a test of mindfulness, perhaps, because it cannot be done quickly or with violence. We must retreat a step, bend a little, turn a shoulder, pinch a green stalk just at a thornless part and peel it carefully away from us without ripping cloth or skin.

There! We are ready again to get going. But after two or three more crackling strides in last year's dry sticks and this year's upsurging weeds, we meet more of these same brambles, whose crooked green stalks, spilling outward, seem to prohibit our going farther. Let us stand here a moment (although the sun is uncomfortably hot) and plot a sensible route, if we can, to the freedom of the woods. This field, we can see, is really not a field anymore in any agricultural sense, still less anyone's yard, but just part of an old farm going wild, just land escaping terminology and sprouting into a thousand forms. The roadside fence is overrun with ivy. There are red cedars and dogwoods and sumacs starting up in inscrutable randomness everywhere in the thick grass. All sorts of shrubs and weeds and saplings are getting going, certainly too crowded for all to survive but trying nonetheless, reaching out in stalk, vine, and leaf under the May sun.

The thorniest and most abundant bramble here is this multiflora rose with green foliage and white flowers on fearsome, barbed stalks—a thickly growing, indefatigably spreading hazard to human wanderers. It looks as though we could just slide past it with a little care, but an incautious touch ensnares us; we get scratched and stuck and worse caught up with every rash movement. We must treat the formidable shrub with respect, and that means backing off and detouring again and again and maybe never getting exactly where we wished to go. It is annoying, but at least it alerts us to some of the roughness in nature. The thorns will discipline us quite seriously until we calm down and pay attention to the moment. This actually might turn out to be good fortune, because our purposes sometimes get in the way of our understanding, whereas chance and frustration, disagreeable as they are, sometimes bring us to a happy collision with truth.

The multiflora rose has broken out in white blossoms—the source, we realize, of the lovely perfume that fills the field. The plant is beautiful to see, beautiful to smell; it obliges us to be mindful; and it turns us toward philosophy. For a short while only we get this curious mingling of beauty and danger; the rest of the year the rose is all danger, even if not a lethal one. So much of nature, when we get down close to it, is spikes and barbs and ingenious hostility. We sigh over landscapes seen through a window but sweat and grumble when actually on foot in the thorny thickets. We have no malice toward the multiflora rose, but the rose will not be disturbed in any case, will not let us pass unchastened through its dominions. Its amazingly sharp thorns seem almost sentient in their propensity to snag us. Still, the plant gives off great sweetness, and the beauty of its flowers pleases us, so we cannot despise it even though it deals us painful scratches.

Nature here and everywhere will not settle into one character and gratify us with predictable sameness—its aspects waver endlessly before us, and we go on pronouncing them good or bad depending on our momentary position. We judge impulsively from self-interest and so judge badly. Somehow we have gotten ourselves wound up in sticky weeds and brambles—wound up in the world's manifold annoyances— and we resent the little curved thorns that hook into our skin, feeling the injury as a personal outrage. But the thorns, considered objectively, are in themselves quite passive and innocent. They cannot cut, they cannot pierce, except as we press upon them. They merely wait, unmoving or at most bobbing faintly with the breeze, until we thrust ourselves in their midst and insist on being scratched. Our sweeping arms and legs do the witless work—until here we are, wincing and muttering and hopping about with plenty of new grievances. But how much of our present misery, we must ask, can we blame on the multiflora rose? And how much of our misfortune elsewhere is the result of our own folly?

Craving, impatience, and self-importance impel us more certainly toward affliction than toward our chosen destinations. While we can run on unimpeded we consider the world good and beautiful, and when we crash into thistles we brood on grimness and failure; but in either case, without the aid of the Dhamma, delusion thrives. What the Dhamma gives us is the means to extract ourselves from brambles or not to get stuck in the first place. The world that we see by turns as attractive or repellent is really just a field of fluctuating, interdependent conditions within which we prosper or suffer according to the wisdom or the folly of our kamma, our own intentional action.

Folly is an effortless accomplishment, but wisdom is always an earned power. To earn it we must reflect with energy on whatever our senses bring us; we must listen respectfully to those who know the world better than we do; and we must train and develop our minds by using—not just admiring—virtue and concentration in our daily business. In the Pāli Canon the vital truths of nature are written down in plain terms, but they can be comprehended only partially until we act in accordance with them. The thorns in the field before us now are certainly no pleasure, but they do furnish us with fruitful metaphors and concrete opportunities for learning. As we warily skirt the flowering, scented masses of multiflora rose, we remember the Dhamma we have read and begin to detect this Dhamma, now vivid and palpable, in those flowers and thorns. If we must detour a long way around to get back on our planned route or must abandon the route altogether, our efforts to be mindful, we need not doubt, are still worthwhile.

Shall we not do our hiking, as well as our thinking, as true philosophers? Since we cannot march straight ahead here, let us retreat some yards and roam unhurriedly through these groves of spindly sumacs, bending where we must, stepping high over upstart shrubs, until we can get ourselves into a free path. What is it to take a walk, anyway? Surely the noblest destinations are not simply geographical. Rambling through the country on a fine day like this, we have an idea, more or less, of where we would like to go—where we might find education or delight—but surely we ought not to be much put out if circumstances oblige us to go elsewhere. A sassafras leaf or a mossy ledge or a stream in sunshine or any other interesting object picked out in the distance will probably serve just as well our higher, unarticulated purpose of reading truth in nature.

Now, look, here is the semblance of a path—maybe just a deer track—twisting away deeper into the field that is really neither field nor forest. We can scrape through here, can't we? What a bristling, sticky, overgrowing inconvenience is nature! And yet what mysteries and what invitations to adventure we find here. The grass brushed back and the ground made barely passable by living creatures suggest to us that we can get through here, too, and maybe make our way to some rare, out-of-the-way knowledge; but unfortunately we are too tall or too ungainly to get along in comfort. We have to stoop and creep and duck under whipping

branches and drooping vines—all the while watching out for brambles—
so that in only a few minutes we are puffing and sweating and in worse
humor. Bugs are whizzing around us, maybe biting, and at every few
steps we seem to walk straight into a spider web. We pick at the half-
seen, elastic strands and ruefully reflect how little it takes to annoy us and
how crowded the world is with annoying things.

How shall we answer annoying things? How shall we answer the worse
pains that fall upon us? Here we are, wandering in a thicket both literal
and figurative, where thorns lurk beneath green foliage, where nature
prodigiously gives birth and kills, where nothing stands secure for more
than a sunny moment, and where, nonetheless, rose perfume still
enchants us. We have grown up confident in human knowledge and
power, supposing ourselves innately capable of understanding and man-
aging life; but in certain revealing hours like these when we have strayed
away from the commotion of civilization, when we have gotten off the
level pavement, we find how tender our skin is, how shaky our step, how
faint our breath, how fragile our poise in the turbulence of nature. Beauty
and death, ease and pain, surround us here; and amid such a blur of conditions can we hope that any track in the grass will lead us where *only*
beauty and ease prevail? If not, how shall we act?

What we glimpse of animal life around us is not uplifting in this
respect. The spiders scampering in their webs are busy trapping and
killing; the woodpeckers in the trees, making a cheerful rhythm, methodically devour small creatures in their hiding places; and far above us the
hawks, we may be sure, are circling with the same hungry purpose. If the
purposes of any of these beings succeed, they do not thereby mount to
any spiritual peace, any superior life that we can see—they just survive in
ignorance a little longer and furnish us, quite inadvertently, with beauty
and with urgent questions.

The response to trouble and affliction that creatures mostly give is
fear, suspicion, hostility, and violence. Of simple charity we see little in
nature—some maternal affection and camaraderie of the pack, but not
much of what we could call disinterested virtue. Mercy is meaningless
where survival is the sovereign imperative. Why is it then that we, mortal creatures possessed of the same primal drives as all others, will even

pause at such a notion as virtue? From the purely biological standpoint, what advantage can there be in any course of behavior that does not promote survival or sensual pleasure?

We muse on inconclusively, aware that, while we remain ardently concerned with material desires, we have not wholly forgotten higher matters and, strangely, do not wish to forget them. We dawdle along, sensitive to occasional inspirations and suspecting, in spite of the world's matter-of-fact cruelty, that there is some kind of virtuous action possible for us as thinking beings that could conduct us past the humdrum of entertainments to a better and worthier goal. Today we are out wandering for health, for the pleasure of the scenery, for relaxation, for relief from worries; but these are only the trifling, conventional reasons that we would tell our neighbors. Beyond these, less certainly, we are groping about in the fields and woods for signs of a path of belief and practice that will answer our secret and unuttered internal need.

The narrow animal trail that we are now attempting to follow is not the sublime path we imagine, yet in its secrecy and wildness it gives us a sense of possibilities out of the ordinary but not hopelessly far away. We who have so long subsisted in square-ruled rooms empty of surprise rejoice in even this slight adventure of working through a thicket in the last, fragrant phase of spring. Abandoning slack habit, we are willing to stagger after fresh perception, to cross boundaries, and to try to learn something of the laws that drive this beautiful and tormented world.

Here, renewed again by sun and rain, there is wild growth accompanied by fierce destruction. Leaf overshadows leaf and creature kills creature while we creep through the greenery in a complicated mood of frustration, fatigue, and hope. Just when the way opens up a little, here is the multiflora rose again, hooking our clothes and recalling us from abstract philosophy. Let us be mindful of the immediate and the concrete, by all means, not losing philosophy but applying it at once to thorns and flowers and all things we directly perceive. Here are not dreams but sensible realities coming into prominence. Is not all of this struggle for food and dominance around us an illustration of the teaching of the Buddha? What do craving and ferocity, however skillful, ultimately achieve but repeated birth, repeated death, repeated ignorance?

What paths can ignorant creatures make or follow except those that lead to food or water or, at best, brief sanctuary in the woods? To escape the thickets of ignorance, to get beyond the realm of old age and death, we need a superior path, a supramundane path, and that is what the Buddha discovered and made known.

In one discourse recorded in the Pāli Canon the Buddha gives the monks the simile of a man wandering in a forest who finds "an ancient path, an ancient road traveled upon by people in the past." That man follows the path and comes upon an ancient, empty city that had been inhabited long ago, "with parks, groves, ponds, and ramparts, a delightful place." He returns to civilization and asks the king of that country to renovate that city. This is accomplished, and in time the beautiful city becomes again prosperous and full of people. The Buddha tells the monks that he himself is like that wanderer in the forest:

> So too, bhikkhus, I saw the ancient path, the ancient road traveled by the Perfectly Enlightened Ones of the past. And what is that ancient path, that ancient road? It is just this Noble Eightfold Path; that is, right view, right intention, right speech, right action, right livelihood, right effort, right mindfulness, right concentration. I followed that path and by doing so I have directly known aging-and-death, its origin, its cessation, and the way leading to its cessation.
>
> (Saṃyutta Nikāya 12:65)

The ancient path leading out of suffering to the highest happiness exists whether or not anybody knows about it, but it is only of use to us if we learn about it and then actually follow it, if we apply its eight factors in our own lives. The Buddha, having directly known birth, aging, and death, and the way out of them, proclaims the trustworthy route to the sublime city of liberation.

The parts or factors of the Noble Eightfold Path are all aspects of individual behavior that can be cultivated by individual will—none, happily, depend on chance or fate. We need to establish right view: the understanding that things happen according to causes, that our actions are significant, that we should respect our parents, that virtuous deeds are worth performing, that the circumstances of our future births will depend on the moral quality of the actions we have done, that this present world is not the only world, and that there are sages in this world who deserve honor. We need right intention; namely, the intention of renunciation of all destructive, defiling things, the intention of harmlessness, and the intention of non-ill will, or good will. Then there is right speech: abstaining from false speech, malicious speech, harsh speech, and gossip. Right action concerns behavior by body: abstaining from killing, from stealing, and from sexual misconduct, and instead practicing harmlessness, respect for the property of others, and honor, faithfulness, and self-restraint in sexual matters. Right livelihood means making a living only by honest and harmless means, not cheating or otherwise hurting any living being. Right effort means striving to forestall or overcome unwholesome states and to arouse and maintain wholesome states. Right mindfulness is clear attention, presence of mind, alertness to what is happening in the present moment, particularly with regard to the body, to feelings, to the mind, and to mental objects. Right concentration is built-up mental concentration, free from sensual obsessions and accompanied by wholesome factors of mind.

Of this grand path, this ancient road in the wilderness, the Buddha says simply and significantly, "I followed that path." It is not enough to hear about it, to imagine its existence out there somewhere in our future; we must undertake to follow it now, and certainly with as much will as we apply to our present, merely physical, activities.

Here we are, stumbling through brambles with the mundane wish of getting to a place where we can walk freely and enjoy the scenery without its scraping over our skin; but the delights and pains of this wild field together with the freshly arisen idea of Dhamma are somehow spurring us to look further for what we could call liberation. Would it not be strange, would it not be wonderful, if all our life-long wanderings, all our tentative explorations of the unaccustomed, have been, at bottom, intuitive attempts to attain liberation? Nothing in the furious sensuality of nature urges quietude or meditation; nothing praises self-denial or charity; nothing extols the overcoming of delusion; yet, with all our fecklessness and frivolity, we are brought to bright attention, we are brought to hope, when we hear the Dhamma in its threefold form of virtue, concentration, and wisdom. The way to the cessation of suffering exists, and it is possible to follow it. Here in this field suddenly rich with metaphors we begin to consider our own strength and what we should do with it.

All the hungry, sun-goaded life around us here is sprouting, consuming, growing, straining not toward any nobility or freedom but toward continuance merely, toward fruit and seed and struggle and death without end. We have long been part of this ignorant passion; but happily now we resist a little, we guess at liberation; and the Buddha's teaching, when at last we listen to it, confirms our best intuition and shows us the right way.

Nature's behest is to capture and devour, to seize what can be seized, but the Buddha teaches us instead to give, to bestow on living beings "five gifts, known from early times, known for long, known by tradition, ancient and unrejected...." These gifts are not material things but actions we can all do, irrespective of our poverty or wealth, that will immeasurably benefit both us and the suffering world:

> Herein, monks, a noble disciple gives up the taking of life and abstains from it. By abstaining from the taking of life, the noble disciple gives to immeasurable beings freedom from fear; he gives freedom from hostility; he gives freedom from oppression. By giving to immeasurable beings freedom from fear, hostility, and oppression, the noble disciple himself will enjoy immeasurable freedom from fear, hostility, and oppression.... Further, monks, a noble disciple gives up the taking of what is not given...gives up sexual misconduct...gives up wrong speech...gives up wine, liquor, and intoxicants that cause negligence. By abstaining...the noble disciple gives to immeasurable beings freedom from fear, hostility, and oppression. By giving to immeasurable beings freedom from fear, hostility, and oppression, the noble disciple himself will enjoy immeasurable freedom from fear, hostility, and oppression.
>
> (Aṅguttara Nikāya 8:39)

If we give up killing, we do in fact confer a great kindness on count-less living beings, because all of them will then be entirely safe in our presence; we will harm none of them; none will need to fear us; we will not engage in hostility or oppression. If we abstain from stealing, nobody will need to fear loss of his property to us; his mind can be at ease on that account. If we abstain from sexual misconduct, nobody will need to fear faithlessness and adultery from us; husband, wife, children, and all fam-ily members will be safe from seduction, sexual abuse, and all other sex-ual indecencies. If we abandon wrong speech and devote ourselves to right speech, friends and strangers alike need have no apprehension that we will trick them or lie to them or speak harshly or maliciously to them—they can count on courteous, honest words from us. If we abstain from taking intoxicants, all people can be sure that we will not harm them or offend them in the stupor of intoxication or damage their property or endanger them by irresponsible, negligent behavior.

Fear, hostility, and oppression are the usual, unsurprising results of unrestrained, selfish actions, whereas peace of mind and freedom from worry are the immeasurable gifts that a person who disciplines himself in the way of Dhamma naturally gives to countless living beings. Such giving, moreover, accumulates to the credit of the giver: by making oth-ers free from fear, hostility, and oppression, he acquires, as the lawful result of his actions, the same freedoms for himself. This is an example of how the Dhamma, being the means for the liberation of the striving individual, is at the same time the means for the increased good fortune and safety of countless other beings. When we work rightly according to Dhamma for our own welfare, our actions cannot help but spill over into other lives, bounteously and beautifully, as the fragrance of wild blossoms spills over the whole field in which they grow.

We are walking now, making such physical motions as other crea-tures make, suffering discomforts of heat and thorns, meditating uno-riginally on hunger, looking out for our advantage, exercising and getting tired without the least uniqueness among the crowds of living things; but we find that we are carrying with us a rare treasure that we are just now beginning to understand—this Dhamma passed down from the Buddha so long ago, amazingly surviving the mischance and oblivion of history until it has lodged in our hearts. What if we were to act toward other beings not as animal instinct urges us but as the Buddha, the Enlightened One, teaches; that is, by giving immeasurable gifts through our own moral discipline? Could we with good practice come to spread fragrance as does the multiflora rose, yet bear no thorns?

Look now, we seem to have lost the trail we were pursuing, but the shade has darkened and we are at last crossing into the coolness of the forest. The undergrowth here is less dense, less thorny, and we can stand straight and walk a little easier, picking our way slowly around heaps of dead wood toward what looks like a clearing ahead. Much rain has made the forest lush and damp, and we peer through an enchanted maze of mossy trees and vines with the hope that we have entered into a landscape more congenial and more fruitful than the one we just left.

But the clearing that attracts us turns out to be not a clearing at all, just a slight thinning in the undergrowth; and as we pause, puffing and blinking and picking off more spider webs, we become aware that the forest, although certainly beautiful, displays at close hand aspects we had forgotten or ignored. We are surrounded not just by big healthy trees and small fresh plants flowering prettily in yellow, purple, and white but also by a vast quantity of unsightly woodland rubbish: fallen dead branches covering the ground and hanging grotesquely in the living branches of saplings, rotten logs everywhere, grayish skeletons of red cedars not yet fallen, dangling shreds of vines, and beneath the living undergrowth a dank waste of sticks, mud, withered weeds, and decomposing leaves. All the growth and flowering that we admire is balanced by disease, decay, and destruction. The graceful beech tree, however tall and grand, in time rots hollow, drops even its great limbs, and is chewed and eaten to ruin. Beneath it, small, shadowed plants live out their season and crumple unbeautifully into the soil. Twigs, leaves, husks, hunks of bark go on falling and accumulating. Growth is followed, is endlessly accompanied, by the dreary shedding of substance, as if no flowering, no achievement at all, will ever stand but must fall to make a base for the next doomed green shoots.

These processes are perfectly ordinary and unsurprising, but we have mostly disregarded them in favor of a narrow, sentimental vision—never actually realized—of forest as eternal paradise, of all untouched nature as free, benign, and lovely. As we stand here catching our breath and squinting against the tiny flying insects, we must, realistically, take stock of the ambivalence of nature and reflect that in the natural run of things we can expect no deliverance from suffering and that even if we should discover here a broad, smooth trail through the woods, that would only ease our afternoon recreation, not lead us where we really need to travel.

So shall we attempt to move on in more ways than one? It is not that, in plodding through the forest, simply covering ground, we will eventually be presented with a scene of culminating, liberating meaning, but rather that, if we walk and listen and observe with care, the changing objects that flash upon our senses will more and more illuminate that true path of virtue, concentration, and wisdom which we must undertake.

We are meandering now, choosing to step left or right just as obstacles appear, and admiring in brief glances the broken green ceiling of forest far above. How much will and energy we have spent just going from one place to another! Shouldn't we at least be able to gather some truth as we go? It is a little cooler here in the forest, to be sure, but the bugs are just as troublesome as out in the sun-blasted field, spider webs are if anything more abundant, and off to either side now we notice wiry green vines, armed with thorns, growing in loose masses. Through them, too, we had best not go.

But the yellow beams of light that break through the leaves, and the swish of a breeze high up, and the tiny, colorful flowers about our feet, and the sweet, damp scent of the forest—couldn't these give us sufficient recompense for the stings of life? Couldn't beauty, albeit temporary, outweigh our fears and griefs? We wish this could be so—we wish it with deep longing—but mindfulness, backed by the wisdom of the Buddha, shows otherwise. A man entering a thorny forest, says the Buddha, would have thorns around him on all sides and would, accordingly, go forward and back mindfully. "So too, bhikkhus, whatever in the world has a pleasing and agreeable nature is called a thorn in the Noble One's Discipline. Having understood this thus as 'a thorn,' one should understand restraint and nonrestraint" (*Saṃyutta Nikāya* 35:244). *Restraint* means the wise discipline of body, speech, and mind that prevents foolish and harmful behavior. *Nonrestraint* means laxness, indulgence, surrender to craving and aversion. The somber truth to be understood here is that pleasing, beautiful, and agreeable things—those things we look to for relief from our troubles—can ensnare and oppress the mind as easily and as fatally as outright miseries. It is wise action alone, individual willed action, that can carry us out of suffering, not any ephemeral disposition of the flickering world.

Which shall we grasp hold of, which shall we seize and treasure—the blossom or the thorn? After we have begun to learn the Dhamma, and after we have roamed for a while with mindfulness in these acres of forest and farm gone wild, the danger in all grasping may become more visible. Blossom and thorn—they are finally the same, for both will ensnare and lacerate the infatuated mind. Does it much matter whether lust drives us or fear drives us, whether we are running toward pleasure or away from pain? Still we are driven, and still it is the same desperate rush of ignorance that finds no end and gains no safety. Here in this realm of birth and death, where all things change and causes everywhere set off effects, what serves us best is action aimed at the good beyond the moment's enjoyment. Restraining all cruelty and greed, forswearing hostility, we can bestow freedom from fear on living beings. By giving thus, by renouncing the craving to lay hold of this or that, we can climb gradually out of the thickets of saṃsāra.

Time gets lost out here in the woods, and we measure it only by the degree of our fatigue or thirst or hunger. Stepping high, striding long or short, balancing in tricky spots, lunging forward again, on we go until, just up ahead where the woods thin out again, we see a swath of bare dirt. Well, finally! Isn't that a trail? We make for it eagerly, staggering through the underbrush, emerging into a band of sunlight. Yes, certainly it is a trail, a nice wide one curving away through a meadow toward more shady woods. Good! Things will soon get easier for us.

But here we have to stop. One long, crooked arc of multiflora rose hangs across our way like a green gate closed before us—one single branch laden with blossoms and sharp, hooked thorns, one last barrier to our anticipated ease. It is nothing to stop us, really, just one curved stalk, waist-high, between us and a smooth trail going left and right into beautiful regions. But what hilarious chance, what lovely symbolism! We must smile, we must marvel and be glad, as the Dhamma pondered over and the land crossed with a careful step have together wrought such meaning for our understanding. We pause, we think it over, and we decide to act.

Come now, brave traveler! Extend your hand, with two fingers or three at most, to touch with concentration a smooth and thornless place on the stalk. Lift it now, most mindfully, steady in the atmosphere of its sweet perfume, careful that it shall not spring suddenly and scratch you. Lift the fierce thorns and enchanting flowers high enough to pass beneath. Now step forward, bend a little, turn with what grace you can, lower the stalk again easily, slowly, down, back to its place. Release it gently and withdraw your hand, and watch it bob harmlessly in the sunlight. There! Turn and go free.

So we are past the simple green gate. We shall not be detained by ugliness or by beauty, and we have found a fine, wide path to travel on. How rich the world is, and has always been, with symbols everywhere to refresh us. But never mind this literal path in the country in the burning depth of May—have we found, or begun to find, that ancient path, that ancient road traveled by the enlightened ones of the past? May it be so. Then somewhere up ahead, through days of thought and work, there lies that ancient, timeless city, undecayed and pure, where aging and death must cease and all afflictions end. Shall we not find it for ourselves? Thorns and blossoms both are pointing out the way.

7. Two Bright States

Not all disagreeable things are bad. Not all unpleasantness is harmful. The truths we must learn and practice to become mature and honorable people may very well cause us discomfort at first as they force us out of the way of habit and onto a challenging trail that leads to a nobler view of the world. Because the teaching of the Buddha is aimed not at superficial, temporary comfort but at release from all suffering, we must pay attention to important things we would rather ignore and exert ourselves when we would rather relax. What is valuable, helpful, and nourishing is sometimes found in the very experiences we instinctively dislike.

The Buddha is a teacher of action, of the power of action. Causes and effects, actions and results, run on everywhere, seen and unseen, rumbling through vast world-systems and wavering through our own day-dreams, making us, remaking us, guiding us, or misguiding us in the long wandering of saṃsāra. Only by understanding the potency of actions and by wisely governing our own behavior can we gain peace and liberation. What we desire in any impulsive moment is one thing; what we ought to do, for the intelligent approach to happiness, may be another. Good guidance is available in the Buddha's recorded words and is reinforced by intuition when we discipline ourselves to listen and observe.

During all periods of our lives disagreeable sensations visit us often, born of various causes, some of which are beyond our control and some not. When we consider doing an action of questionable moral quality—

anything that makes us flinch and worry—we usually give some thought (although it might not be very deep) to what others will think of the action or what we ourselves will think of it in the future. We measure the planned deed against the standards of society or our own internal standards, such as they are; we imagine bad consequences; we consider the likelihood of blame, punishment, or guilt that we might incur. Intentionally or involuntarily, we test desire against conscience. When conscience is weak or unclear, we might go ahead with what we want to do, and then we will encounter in lawful course, and sometimes with sharp surprise, the natural results of our behavior. Whether we will *know* these results for what they are is an open question. Whether we will understand the dynamic sequence of desire, intention, action, and result is likewise an uncertain, variable matter that depends on our education in the Dhamma and our keenness of observation.

When, for whatever reason, we determine to carry out some questionable plan, we discover that our intentions and actions raise a pungent cloud of emotions around them. We may be touched by excitement, fear, satisfaction, depression, or guilt, among other sensations, often in a different or more intense way than we had anticipated. Because these sensations are not always pleasant or manageable, we try over time to build around ourselves some kind of philosophy for protection or else to adopt whatever expedients our friends seem to use for consolation. By some obscure process of collective accommodation and agreement, certain ideas periodically become prominent in the world and hence attractive and powerful if we have nothing better to rely on. Whether they are true or not is something we ought to look into.

The headlong pursuit of pleasure or self-gratification so common in prosperous modern society has as its necessary and comfortable support the assumption that we need not, must not, be *ashamed,* that as autonomous individuals we should be quite free, quite bold, and quite unapologetic in all our wants. Self-justification, it would seem, is the only justification required—and that is easily obtained. We are susceptible to feelings of shame, and because shame is unpleasant and an impediment to enjoyment, we are at pains to evade it, either by avoiding worrisome and suspect actions or—in keeping with the brazen spirit of the age—by lunging onward with assertions of our freedom and sweet prerogative.

What a dreary and depressing sensation this thing shame is! How antiquated is the notion that we should regret what is only natural appetite! How absurd to allow unwarranted doubts to hamper us! If only we could agree among ourselves *not* to consider shameful those things that were formerly thought so, and, more than that, if we could sufficiently strengthen our conviction of our personal rightness, shouldn't we be able to get rid of this detestable sense of shame, this holdover from a gloomier age? So we sometimes tell ourselves, struggling against a conscience we thought we had tamed.

But still, when we think over a dubious deed we have rushed through, or when we hear a rebuke from someone we respect, we feel the stings, subtle or sharp, of what we can only call shame. Then too, when we think over some dubious plan of ours for the future, or in uneasy retrospection assess what bad things we may have already done, another disagreeable sensation may arise: fear. For all our breezy skepticism, for all our willingness to be careless as the world around us is careless, we continue to sense that there might be, in this life or a life to come, painful consequences to our actions; and that thought, in the lulls of our self-confidence, is upsetting, even frightening—although we might doggedly insist, as brisk, modern individualists, that there is no reason to worry.

Fear of physical harm or emotional upset or financial loss seems quite natural, but why should we feel fear of a moral sort? We are troubled by this experience, for we have absorbed another prevalent belief of our time: that once we have decided for ourselves that an action is justifiable (as far as *we* are concerned), and once we have talked ourselves into a state of confidence, then no possible harm can follow; no moral retribution can touch us. Fear of doing moral wrong is, like shame, so disagreeable that we automatically consider it a weakness, a stain, a defect of irrational origin. We see no good in it and are embarrassed that we, who should have overcome all such doubts, nevertheless keep having to pile up reasons why we are right and justified and immune to any bad effects in the future. Fear about the future results of our deeds, we try to believe, is only a reprehensible ghost that should be summarily dispatched by a resolute person.

The Buddha, however, has a different, quite striking view of these same sensations of shame and fear. He says of them, "These two bright states protect the world" (*Aṅguttara Nikāya* 2:9). They are not always afflictions or weaknesses, but rather, when called up by moral doubt and wisely attended to, they become defenders of the good, guardians of peace, and guides to the achievement of a noble life. How could this be so? Without education in the Dhamma, we naturally assume that what is unpleasant and troublesome can have no value at all and that feelings of shame and fear must always betoken some ugly failing on our part. We would rather *not* fail; we would rather *not* endure any kind of discomfort if it can be warded off with distractions or forgetfulness or hearty self-justification. To tolerate shame and fear seems to us just a weakness of will—for will, nicely private, personal, and independent, is what we admire and prefer to contemplate, rather than any impersonal, impassive law of action and result. But the Buddha says that a sense of shame and fear of wrongdoing are blameless qualities that result in happiness and lead to rebirth in heavenly worlds.

Here we must understand that the terms the Buddha uses—*hiri* and *ottappa*—refer respectively to particular kinds of shame and fear: shame at the thought of doing evil, being burdened with evil, and suffering the disapproval of the wise, and fear of wrongdoing—fear of the actual, painful consequences of unwholesome kamma. We ought not to be ashamed of ordinary, mundane disadvantages, such as being poor, or lacking education, social prominence, beauty, or any number of conventionally admired characteristics, talents, and accomplishments. And we ought not to be ashamed of failing in any particular task or competition when we have made a good effort—triumphs are not a certainty for us in this world, and that is just a fact to recognize and accept with equanimity. What is important, what is truly significant in this realm of cause and effect, is the moral quality of our behavior, our kamma. It is entirely good and right to maintain a sense of shame regarding the actions we are inclined to do—a sense of modesty, reserve, and honor that will alert us to dangers before they can overwhelm us. It is also good and right to maintain a sense of fear, prudence, or wariness toward those tendencies in ourselves and those unworthy deeds we sometimes contemplate that might bring after them painful, grievous results.

A sense of shame benefits us because it reminds us of the ideals of the Dhamma—harmlessness, self-control, dignity, honesty, kindness, and other virtues that otherwise might remain abstractions remote from our daily living. All of us wish to be able to see ourselves as respectable or at least as striving honorably to give better shape to our character; so when we cultivate and heed this sense of shame we gain valuable reminders of the decent limits to our behavior and of the picture of our character that we display. How are we perceived? How are we judged by others? How do we secretly judge ourselves? Such reflections nudge us toward safe ground. When we transgress a moral precept a little or much, that burning, that inner sting of shame, bad as it may feel, is not something to be smothered and forgotten but rather an important sign to be attended to, for it shows the good working of our conscience. Without it we would be in a much worse condition.

A sense of fear of wrongdoing benefits us, too, because it reminds us of the universal law of action and result, which defers to nobody and which functions with absolute impartiality, silently conducting us into an appropriate future. Every day we conceive and put forth intentional actions of various kinds, and these will have effects on us. Our forgetfulness and our wish that certain actions will just pass away will have no influence over this mighty law. Thus, when we have learned something of the good Dhamma and when we feel fear, apprehension, or mistrust over some action we intend, we are actually hearing a salutary alarm, a call to remember our principles. Apart from the pain of seeing frowns on the faces of those we respect, and apart from the stark picture of ourselves that we must contemplate and cannot avoid, there is the fact that unwholesome actions can and do bring about all sorts of outright pain, degradation, and wretchedness for those who do such actions. Like all other beings, we are heirs of our own actions, both the good and the bad, so we certainly need to pay attention to what sort of potential we are building up for the future.

These fundamental principles of action are not hard to grasp. We are anxious about our own welfare and capable of understanding that the deeds we do will leave their traces upon us and that a sense of shame and a sense of fear and revulsion toward evil can protect us from folly. But why, we might wonder, does the Buddha say that these states "protect the world"? This is because what is good for us—good for our own well-being in the present and in the future—is also good for other living beings. Our behavior affects them. A person who does not try to run away from a sense of shame but rather makes earnest efforts at self-control necessarily and naturally spreads light, beauty, and peace around him. Such a person, conscientiously attending to the improvement of his own character, will not harm other living beings. Thus other living beings are always safe in his presence. No one needs to fear violence, theft, sexual misconduct, or other mistreatment at his hands, for he will be ashamed of such things, will reject any vicious ideas, and will instead perform deeds of kindness and charity. It is a matter of honor and a matter of understanding as well.

Furthermore, such a person, remembering the Buddha's explanations of the workings of kamma, and observing for himself the dire suffering into which heedless beings can fall, will maintain a stout, wholesome sense of fear, caution, and presence of mind with regard to evil deeds. Clearly distinguishing good from evil, he will lean toward the good and shun the evil simply as a practical matter of preserving his own well-being, in addition to expressing whatever altruism and friendliness he has cultivated in his practice of Dhamma. Thus such a person protects the world both by his self-restraint regarding what is unwholesome and by his earnest performance of what is good and likely to bring good results to himself and others. One who does not regard himself as immune to the consequences of evil and who respects the law of kamma gives unlimited protection to everyone around him simply by protecting his own welfare.

The Buddha calls shame and fear of wrongdoing "bright states" and says that one who possesses them lives happily. They have nothing to do with gloomy, obsessive anxieties about indefinite matters in the future, or with sickly remorse regarding unrecoverable past deeds. In the teaching of the Buddha shame at the thought of dishonorable behavior and fear of wrongdoing and its consequences are decidedly healthy qualities that are "without affliction." Here as always it is helpful to remember that as a teacher of the power of action, the Buddha frequently explains how good things are brought about through the combination, accumulation, and development of specific, wholesome conditions. These bright states of shame and fear, despite the superficial alarm that accompanies them, are wholesome conditions that tend to ripen in beautiful and useful ways—thus they should be cultivated.

Even if all our relatives or friends or all the world should agree in some case that there are no grounds for shame and that self-satisfaction is the only criterion for sensible action, that would have no effect whatever on the great law of action and result. We will still feel a secret burning whenever we depart from the noble principles we instinctively respect. It is just the way the human mind works; and the Buddha, who understands the human mind, trains his followers to watch over their minds and heed these good warnings of intuition.

For the monks in particular the Buddha sets a strict standard. On one occasion he asks them whether they would feel "hurt, ashamed, and repelled" if followers of other teachings should ask them if they practiced the Dhamma just for the sake of being reborn in a heavenly world. The monks—who know very well that their duty as members of the Sangha is to strive much further, for liberation from *all* suffering—reply that they would indeed feel hurt, ashamed, and repelled at such a question. Then the Buddha bids them consider the implications of their feelings:

> So then, monks, you seem to feel hurt, ashamed, and repelled by divine life-span, divine beauty, divine bliss, divine glory, and divine sovereignty. How much more then should you feel hurt, ashamed, and repelled by wrong conduct in deeds, words, and thoughts!
>
> (Aṅguttara Nikāya 3:18)

These monks would be mortified if others thought their practice was aimed at what is, compared with Nibbāna, a relatively low goal; but the Buddha wishes them to realize that if they would be upset over the misunderstanding of others, and if they would recoil even from the glories of the (impermanent) heavenly worlds, then they should recoil much more from actual bad conduct. One's own bad deeds, words, and thoughts are the most dangerous ills, and of these one should rightly be ashamed.

Even if everyone around us should confidently tell us that all we need to do in some situation is to decide on what personally seems right to us and all will be well, and even if we should enthusiastically agree and be convinced, that would have no effect on the impersonal workings of kamma. An intentional action by way of body, speech, or mind will produce results according to the "root" of that action. If the root (beneath all euphemism, forgetfulness, and self-deception) is really greed, hatred, or delusion, if we are fundamentally intending harm, then unpleasant, unhappy results can be expected, regardless of our wish for something better. If we desire, for whatever reason, to kill or rob or do other harm to living beings, that desire, being intrinsically unwholesome, ensures that the consequent actions and results will be unwholesome.

Safety in this world and beyond requires that we respect and heed the laws of nature. However much we may prosper, however strong and confident we may be, there are, according to the Buddha, four things that no one at all in the universe can do. No one can prevent what is subject to decay from decaying. No one can prevent what is subject to sickness from falling sick. No one can prevent what is subject to death from dying. And no one can prevent evil, impure actions from having their grave and painful results.

However we might wish the universe to be different from what it is, no gesture of our will, no power of ours at all, can stop the tremendous current of causality. No one turns it back. The force of a pure or an impure deed resounds through time and ripens according to its potency, and the wise do not pretend that their opinions can alter its nature. They know their actions will flourish, that fruit will follow seed lawfully, so they gracefully adapt themselves to the law of action and conscientiously do good. Their pure and honorable deeds will have effects of which no one can deprive them.

No matter what we tell ourselves or contrive to believe, certain deeds are inherently impure and destructive and cannot be neutralized by any clever reasoning. For example, nowadays much of society, careless of the principle of cause and effect, sees abortion and euthanasia as acceptable means to desired personal ends; but abortion and euthanasia remain forms of intentional killing that can never be other than bad and can never be reconciled with the Buddha's message of harmlessness and sympathy. Compassion for the helpless should deter us from all such deeds, supported by shame at the thought that our devotion to harmlessness could be nothing but words, and reinforced by very serious respect for the power of bad kamma.

Acts of injuring or killing living beings arise from unwholesome roots and produce suffering for those who do the acts. It is the same with stealing and sexual misconduct and all forms of cruelty, abuse, false speech, and dishonesty. Unwholesome actions are not all of the same gravity, but they all share the same nature of giving rise to future misfortune. Communities and societies variously decide what they will condemn and what not, as matters of custom or law; but still the thoughtful individual, mindful of the Dhamma, must make his or her own, and perhaps stricter, moral decisions based on an understanding of deeper principles, not relying merely on chance, fashion, or the habits of the multitude. Shamelessness and disregard for the effects of wrongdoing put us in the way of great suffering, for they predispose us to commit bad kamma and thus to receive the appropriate results of that kamma; but shame and fear of wrongdoing, well heeded and learned from, conduct the virtuous person to the heavenly planes.

Even if shame comes upon us as a result of bad deeds we have already done, we ought not to think we are permanently defiled and ruined. Conditions will always change, and they can change for the good if we take the right steps. Shame reminds us of the moral ideals we have forgotten and moves us to correct ourselves. Seeing honestly where we have erred, and admitting it to ourselves, we should strive all the more diligently to do good. Then our kindly and virtuous actions may in time build up and outweigh the bad. All effects of kamma, as it happens, eventually become exhausted and disappear; so if we distinctly recognize past wrongdoing and do not repeat it, and if we go on to do good zealously and without ceasing, we can expect our suffering to wane in time and our happiness to increase. The Buddha, speaking to monks remorseful over various offenses, often says this:

Surely, bhikkhu, you have committed a transgression…. But since you see your transgression as a transgression and make amends for it in accordance with the Dhamma, we pardon you for it. For it is growth in the Noble One's Discipline when one sees one's transgression as a transgression, makes amends for it in accordance with the Dhamma, and undertakes future restraint.

(Aṅguttara Nikāya 9:11)

The principle is good for lay people, too. Although lay people need not do any formal confession as monks do, it is certainly necessary, for our relief and our future comfort, to admit to ourselves when we have done wrong and to determine to behave more worthily henceforth. Humbly acknowledging a transgression does not annul the transgression—it does not wipe out its effects—but it does help us to get back on the right moral course and gives us fresh strength to restrain ourselves and act honorably in the future.

This restraint that the Buddha continually urges should not be looked upon as any kind of trial or privation. Good practices and worthy states of mind should instead be esteemed as blessings and riches. Among the various kinds of wealth to be found in the world, there are, the Buddha says, seven kinds of "noble wealth": the wealth of faith, the wealth of virtue, the wealth of shame, the wealth of fear of wrongdoing, the wealth of learning, the wealth of generosity, and the wealth of wisdom. It is instructive to find shame and fear in this list together with other qualities of obvious worth. None of these kinds of wealth, we should note, concern the ephemeral prizes and sensual pleasures of the world. These seven good things, whether recognized by anyone or not, are blessings, true forms of wealth, and marks of spiritual prosperity. They are reliable conditions, available and accessible to all of us, for the destruction of sorrow and the attainment of liberation.

If we feel shame at the thought of an ugly deed and are thereby kept from doing it, shouldn't we rejoice? If presentiments of suffering dissuade us from behaving badly, shouldn't we be justly glad? We who stagger among countless dangers in the wilderness of saṃsāra can find these lamps and profit by their timely light. With regard to all ignoble and unworthy deeds, we do good for ourselves and for others when we observe dispassionately and train ourselves in modesty and self-control. This is the good and gladdening work of Dhamma. We may not always be praised for it—we may even be laughed at—but what does that matter? Let the world laugh and make its feckless pronouncements—but let us live with honor and the beauty of honor.

8. Our Next Destination

IT MIGHT BE ON A WINTER NIGHT, when we look out a window on a bleak landscape; or it might be on a radiant summer day, when we are strolling on a long, broad path in a forest; or it might be in an unexpected moment on city pavement, when we have paused to muse on the flow of people around us. At any time, almost, and from inscrutable causes, the ordinary murmur in our minds can give way suddenly to one special doubt. All things around us are changing, perishing, passing, going out of sight, going on to an unperceivable future; and we are going on, too, going on most certainly to death—and then to where? We who survey the changing human panorama and distantly note the phases of nature are ourselves sliding out of this present life and toward some state of being or non-being or some kind of destination that we do not know but desperately wish to know.

The details of death itself we might be able to imagine and even accept in imagination—the ending of all mundane affairs, the farewells, the progressive failing of the physical systems, the pains and discomforts, the last subsiding of consciousness. But no stoic resolution can ever stifle the ancient, unsettling question: What happens next? Even if we have persuaded ourselves, intellectually, that nothing at all happens next, we cannot refrain from dizzy cogitations on what *might* happen. It is in the nature of the human being to speculate, and to speculate most earnestly on those matters that cannot be settled quickly by evidence near at hand. The universe answers us nothing; we talk to ourselves and get nowhere; we tell ourselves it doesn't matter; but still we want to know and still we will seek knowledge wherever we can, consulting the doctrines of philosophies and religions until we find something that sounds true according to our reason and our taste. If we cannot learn *exactly* what is in store for us, we must have at least a general explanation of the aftermath of death.

In this matter, as in all profound philosophical matters, we waver between faith in our own intuition and faith in wisdom outside ourselves. It is a truism that reliable knowledge must come by way of our own experience; but this truism cannot bear too much weight. It would be satisfying, of course, personally to confirm every fact we have learned about the world by a nice inspection of the phenomenon in question; but since that is impossible, and since our own experience is minuscule with respect to all possible experience, we must rely for most of our practical understanding on the knowledge that external authorities give us. Nearly all of us accept without difficulty the basic propositions of mathematics, physics, geography, and many other disciplines, although we ourselves probably have not the slightest personal acquaintance with, let us say, the structure of atoms or the functioning of stars. We have perceived none of that through our own senses. We depend on authorities for our elementary knowledge and do not think ourselves overly credulous. Thus it would be curious if, on the subject of rebirth, we should turn rigidly skeptical and declare fictitious whatever is beyond our immediate sight. Practically everything, when it comes to that, is beyond our immediate sight.

When we were small children we relied mostly on our parents for information about the world. We had no means then to ascertain the truth of what they told us about sky, earth, ocean, and the creatures that lived around us; but that, quite naturally, did not trouble us at all. Understanding that our parents loved us and wished us well, we were content to take what they told us as facts to rely on until such time as we were grown and able to investigate on our own. Many things they told us did soon prove true in our childish, domestic experience, so we were quite willing to accept, at least provisionally, their descriptions of the wider universe.

Even on into adult life we have easily adopted and made use of countless doctrines of science and art without delving personally into every detail. Even in our own chosen spheres of business or avocation, where we study and learn as directly as we can, we still have relied on teachers to set us going in the right direction, to correct our errors, and to encourage us to attain competence and maturity. In religion as much as in any secular subject this is entirely sensible. If we choose our authorities with care, seeing that they are honorable and wise and concerned for our well-being, and if we do not neglect to exercise our own judgment upon what we are taught, we can proceed quite reasonably to a better comprehension of the universe.

For a Buddhist, needless to say, the best authority on the great question of death and its aftermath is the Buddha himself, who decided to teach in the first place out of compassion for the suffering of living beings. It is not unreasonable to suppose, when we read the Pāli Canon or simply wonder how much faith to put in various Buddhist doctrines, that the Buddha and the sages who followed him knew things that ordinary people did not, and that our vanity should not prevent us from taking in and giving respectful attention to what they have said. We do not see beyond the barrier of bodily death, but we can listen to instruction on the subject from those we respect and then decide how well that accords with what we can perceive in the processes of nature around us.

The Buddha teaches that all phenomena in the universe proceed by way of cause and effect: they arise and pass away not fortuitously, not by meaningless chance, but according to the presence or absence of necessary conditions. Like all other living beings around us, we have come into this particular world, into this particular form of existence, as a result of prior conditions, and unless we attain full enlightenment we can expect that conditions now obtaining will send us on after death to yet another life in this world or another world. The most important of the conditions that affect us is our own intentional action, our kamma. Action accumulates, and its built-up character at the time of our death is what determines our next destination—a destination that may be good or bad, pleasant or unpleasant, but that is also always temporary, sure to give way in time to further death and rebirth unless enlightenment at some point stops the mortal momentum.

It is important to understand, however, that when talking about rebirth the Buddha is not talking about the literal reconstitution of the "same" person in one life after another. A person, strictly speaking, is not an embodied ego but a dynamic combination of five groups or aggregates *(khandhas)*: material form; pleasant, unpleasant, and neutral feeling; perception; mental formations; and consciousness—altogether a process, not a static thing, a stream of phenomena flowing on and turning this way and that according to changing conditions. The persons we know and see are real enough; they are just not absolute, unchanging personalities. For all of us, the life we experience at any moment is the consequence of what went before and will be the impetus for what comes next. The infant gives rise to the child and the child to the adolescent and the adolescent to the adult; and although we may use one personal name to cover this process throughout an observable lifetime, it is still a process, in which the child can never be exactly identified with the adult, nor the adult of one year with the adult of the next. One stage simply provides conditions for the succeeding stage. From one year to the next, even from one moment to the next, a gradual change occurs. Rebirth is only one more conditioned event in the continuing sequence. The dying person gives rise to the living embryo in the womb, and saṃsāra, the cycle of birth and death, continues to turn.

When the Buddha discusses death and its aftermath, then, he is not speaking in the literal-minded way of nearly everyone else. The world at large, in our time as well as in the Buddha's time, wavers between two extreme, wrong doctrines, insisting that truth must be found in one or the other. One is the eternalist doctrine *(sassatavāda)*, which holds that this present, existing person will survive after death, will continue, will go on, more or less intact, to take up residence here or there in the future. The other is the annihilationist doctrine *(ucchedavāda)*, which holds that this present, existing person will be annihilated at death—destroyed, wiped out, obliterated—and there will be no future existence of any kind. We might at first think, "Well, either we survive or we perish—there's no other alternative." But the Buddha rejects both eternalism and annihilationism, because both of them depend on the unspoken assumption that there actually exists a discrete, delimitable self or ego that can survive or be destroyed. Since no such self or ego can be found in the first place—only a flux of empty conditions—to assert its future survival or destruction is meaningless.

We find in the Pāli Canon that when the Buddha is asked questions about death and rebirth that presuppose such a self, he does not side either with eternalism or with annihilationism. Instead, he expounds the deep and subtle doctrine of dependent origination *(paṭicca-samuppāda)*. All living beings are dependently arisen; they exist and change as patterns of conditions dependent upon other conditions. Life does indeed go on from one existence to another, but it is not *identical* life—it is just the natural consequence or outcome of what has gone before.

In the most general terms, living beings, overwhelmed by ignorance *(avijjā)* of the Four Noble Truths and consequently misunderstanding the world they see around them, engage in volitional formations *(saṅkhāras)* of good or bad or indifferent quality. That is to say, out of ignorance they commit actions. These accumulated actions have a result after death: they give rise to renewed consciousness *(viññāṇa)* in some world or other; and the nature of that consciousness is determined by the moral quality of those actions. With consciousness as a foundation or condition, the complex of mental and material factors *(nāmarūpa)*—literally "name and form"—comes to be, providing the conditions in turn for the activity of the six sense bases *(saḷāyatana)* of eye, ear, nose, tongue, body, and mind. When the senses function there is contact *(phassa)*—the coincidence or meeting of the internal sense faculty, the external sense object, and the consciousness of the event. Contact in turn conditions feeling *(vedanā)*, which may be pleasant or unpleasant or neither-pleasant-nor-unpleasant. Dependent on feeling, craving *(taṇhā)* arises. Craving in turn conditions clinging *(upādāna)* to various objects in the perceived world. This clinging drives on the elemental process of becoming or existence *(bhava)*, the endless function of actions producing results. Those actions, still proceeding from ignorance, again bring about birth *(jāti)*; and when there is birth, there follow aging, death, sorrow, lamentation, pain, dejection, and despair *(jarā-maraṇaṃ soka-parideva-dukkha-domanassa-upāyāsa)*.

This is the way life normally runs for living beings, but the Buddha calls it "the wrong way." It is the wrong way because it is an endless cycling that brings suffering and more suffering as a matter of course. The right way, by contrast, comes about when an individual so disciplines himself as to destroy the ignorance that renews and sustains suffering. With the "remainderless fading away and cessation of ignorance," all the factors that depend on ignorance must fail and collapse, until birth itself is no longer produced, and with the cessation of birth there follows the cessation of aging, death, sorrow, lamentation, pain, dejection, and despair—in short, the whole frightful, immemorial burden of suffering. This is the highest liberation, the supreme happiness—Nibbāna.

In all this succession of conditions, whether leading to Nibbāna or only to repeated birth, death, and suffering, no permanent, literal ego or self can be found operating—only the flow of causes and effects. The "person" that we are accustomed to taking as a static fact is really a volatile pattern of conditions, changing even from moment to moment, to which the world attaches a single name. Thus the doctrine of rebirth in Buddhism is a good deal more complex than we might at first assume. A person who is reborn in any world is not identical with a previous person who has died; nor is he or she an entirely new creation. Rather, the relationship is one of continuing conditionality. The reborn person is yet one more phase in the stream of dependent origination.

It is important to understand that although the working of death and rebirth and indeed all of life is in Buddhist teaching a relentless process of causality, it is not a deterministic process. That is to say, nobody is determined or fated to undergo just such-and-such a series of experiences indefinitely into the future, going on and on hopelessly forever. In every moment of consciousness there is present the factor of volition (cetanā): we choose to do this and not to do that; we decide and act in various ways, and thus in effect we steer the current of our existence (deliberately or unwittingly) in one direction or another. This power of volition is what makes possible spiritual advancement and finally enlightenment.

Once we have a preliminary understanding of what a person really consists of and how events are shaped and conditioned by other events, we can go on to consider rebirth in more than a superficial way. It is perfectly correct to say that so-and-so dies and is reborn according to the character of his or her accumulated actions, so long as we bear in mind that what is happening is not the recurrence of any literal ego, self, or absolute identity but just the meandering through time of an ever-changing stream of causes and effects. Whether we use technical terms like "conditions" or as a matter of convenience use names and refer to "persons" or "beings," nature still functions in a dynamic, lawful way. Actions have consequences that may extend beyond the limits of a single lifetime. As long as the momentum of ignorance persists, as long as greed, hatred, and delusion are not entirely eradicated, birth, with its troubles, is produced again in some appropriate plane of existence.

What then, according to Buddhism, are the future possibilities for someone who dies in this world? In the Pāli Canon we find mention of many planes of existence in which living beings may be reborn. These are broadly grouped into the hell plane, the animal plane, the plane of ghosts (petas), the human plane, and the divine plane. As a result of performing certain kinds of actions, one can be reborn in a world in any of these categories, to experience the particular conditions there for a short or a long time, but not forever. Violence, cruelty, dishonesty, and greed lead downward and tend to result in birth in miserable, painful circumstances, whereas harmlessness, kindness, honesty, and generosity lead upward to birth in pleasant, even heavenly, conditions.

The migration of living beings goes on—and has been going on without beginning—entirely according to the natural process of cause and effect. Certain kinds of intentional action, such as killing, stealing, committing sexual misconduct, and telling lies, when indulged in sufficiently, turn the stream of one's existence downward and make rebirth in a miserable world more likely, while refraining from those misdeeds and cultivating their opposites turn the stream of one's existence upward to happier worlds.

When the Buddha finally reached full enlightenment, he remembered his own past births: one, ten, a hundred, a thousand, a hundred thousand, and "many eons of world contraction and expansion"—but nowhere, significantly, any first birth, any beginning to the cycle. On

that epic morning of enlightenment the Buddha also turned his mind to
the "passing away and reappearance of beings" and beheld them migrat-
ing on from life to life:

> *I understood how beings fare on according to their actions thus:*
> *"These beings who engaged in misconduct of body, speech, and mind,*
> *who reviled the noble ones, held wrong view, and undertook actions*
> *based on wrong view, with the breakup of the body, after death, have*
> *been reborn in a state of misery, in a bad destination, in the nether*
> *world, in hell; but these beings who engaged in good conduct of body,*
> *speech, and mind, who did not revile the noble ones, who held right*
> *view, and undertook actions based on right view, with the breakup*
> *of the body, after death, have been reborn in a good destination, in*
> *a heavenly world."*
>
> (Majjhima Nikāya 4:29)

Here then was the foundation of the Buddha's moral teaching—his
direct vision of how cause and effect naturally follow one upon the
other, producing the suffering or happiness that living beings experience. Our next destination in saṃsāra does not depend simply on what
we *wish* will happen; nor is it a matter of meaningless chance; nor is it
fixed by some inscrutable fate. Rather it will be the result of the causes
that we put in place by our actions throughout our lives. Certain kinds
of actions produce misery by their nature; other kinds give rise to good
fortune and happiness. The accumulation of actions eventually directs
the stream of our existence into an appropriate new sphere; so we
should by all means pay good attention to the Buddha's moral cautions
and exhortations.

When we do pay attention we may be struck by some teachings that
run quite counter to the fashion of our time. For those of us who have
grown up with a measure of prosperity and comfort, it seems quite natural to suppose that our next destination, assuming there is one, must be
one of equal or better prosperity and comfort. Although we observe
plenty of suffering and disaster around us, we expect that our own movement through time and fortune will necessarily be upward—to eternal

peace and joy or at least to superior enjoyment in a future state. It is very disagreeable to contemplate a downward movement, not to mention any kind of hell. It is even a little jarring to hear that we are conditioned by our actions in any definite degree and that we cannot overrule the history of our behavior by a simple aspiration or an assertion of our preference.

Although we are quietly, privately hoping for reassurance, for support for our extravagant hopes, the Buddha presents us with a troubling vision of a universe in which suffering abounds, in which not everybody attains to safety and delight, in which actions bring lawful consequences for all beings, and in which there is no attainment of liberation apart from diligent work along the Noble Eightfold Path. All events, good and bad, depend on conditions; and therefore all beings concerned for their own welfare should gather wholesome conditions and avoid the unwholesome. If we fail to do what is necessary to promote our welfare and instead fall into habitual wrongdoing, we can expect bad consequences in this life and in lives to come.

But even if we can understand the basics of kamma and its results, we might still be reluctant to acknowledge the possibility of very bad results, such as rebirth in a hell. It seems so harsh, so severe, so shocking and frightening. A heaven, by contrast, we can imagine. The existence of heavens seems to us for some reason much more likely (and a great deal easier on the imagination); but logically we cannot give credence to heavens without taking into account hells. If good deeds lead on to good destinations, must not bad deeds lead on to bad? This is exactly what the Buddha teaches. The Buddha, we should remember, did not preside over the fates of creatures; he had no power to relieve them of the consequences of their actions. All he could do—and did—was to embody the good way of Dhamma, to teach it, and to urge living beings to follow it for their own good and the good of all.

Living beings are free to exercise their faculty of volition—they are able to choose and they do choose—and they develop or deteriorate because of their actions, moving now up, now down, through the great range of worlds. When actions are good enough, when virtues are built up, there will be rebirth in one of the higher planes of existence that we would call a heaven; and when actions grow sufficiently evil, there will be rebirth in a correspondingly wretched plane of existence—in a hell or in the animal world or in the miserable world of the *petas,* or ghosts. There may also be birth again in this human world, in relatively good or relatively bad circumstances, according to the quality of accumulated past actions.

When someone has finished this present life, and has been reborn in any of these good or bad worlds, there is still no conclusion to the cycle of saṃsāra; there is still no final triumph or irreparable disaster. Life in the beautiful heavenly realms or in the frightful hell realms may be enormously long—many eons—but it is still impermanent. Old age and death manifest themselves at length, followed by passing away and re-arising once again in a new state of existence. The current of causality tumbles on through time, changing and changing but finding no rest. We may fear—as well we should—the possibility of birth as an animal or a being in hell, and we may long for the comforts of heaven; but neither extreme of sentient existence is absolute and eternal, and neither would be the end of our wandering. It is possible to rise from the lower worlds, and it is possible to fall from the higher ones: our piled-up actions will engender appropriate results, both good and bad. While ignorance still reigns in the heart, while greed, hatred, and delusion still exist in the slightest measure, there will always be something further to come, always a next destination ahead.

Thus the Buddha declares that *all* formations are dukkha—unsatisfactory, suffering. This does not mean that birth in the divine worlds or in this human world is not worthwhile—it surely is—but that, because these states are impermanent, they are flawed and should not be viewed as the final goal of religious striving. Taking a longer, philosophical view, we should realize that we cannot rely on any impermanent state for our deliverance. Even the glories and comforts of the divine worlds break down; the beings there run out their life spans and must move on, still not free from the peril of falling into lower realms; so if we are looking for absolute freedom and happiness we must practice not only the cultivation of virtue, not only the accumulation of meritorious deeds, but also the gradual removal from our minds of all vestiges of greed, hatred, and delusion.

The reason that birth in this human plane (which is by no means the highest and purest realm of existence) is especially valuable is that as human beings endowed with a measure of intelligence we experience both misery and pleasure; we observe disasters and triumphs; we become acquainted with tears and laughter—in short, we meet with contrasts that ought to stimulate us to religious effort. Generally speaking, things in this world are not so bad that we will absolutely despair, and they are not so good that we can relax and be entirely free of fear. We exist in tension, in imbalance, in philosophical uncertainty that makes us search for higher truths.

The human plane, moreover, is where Buddhas are born, where they achieve supreme enlightenment, and where they teach the Dhamma for the relief and happiness of many. Living in this human plane in a bright (and brief!) age when the Dhamma is known and available for study and practice, we have right now a beautiful opportunity to start to raise ourselves out of the beginningless cycle of birth and death. Buffeted by contrasts, speculating on the mysteries of death and the imperfections of life, we find encouraging explanations in the teaching of the Buddha. We learn that we are not hopeless, futile motes but dynamic streams of existence capable of rising into nobler states and even attaining Nibbāna, "the unborn supreme security from bondage." We learn, besides, that there is a way accessible to us in this world—the Noble Eightfold Path— by which we can act for our own good. We need not wait eternally for good luck, for the magical disappearance of our troubles, for some fantastic, fortuitous blossoming of happiness. Cause and effect, rightly attended to, will naturally bring blessings.

As we ponder the principle of causality, hoping to obtain blessings and wondering how it is that we have gotten ourselves into our particular troubles in this present life and how we might get out of them in the future, it is helpful to look a little deeper into the process that the Buddha outlines in his teaching on dependent origination. What has thus far prevented us from doing right? What has kept us going around and around in saṃsāra so long? What must we conquer to prevent miserable rebirths in the future? The first factor in the series that the Buddha cites is ignorance—that pernicious blankness, misapprehension of the

nature of the universe, incomprehension of the Four Noble Truths—
and throughout his teaching he emphasizes the significance of ignorance
for the practice of the Dhamma:

> *Bhikkhus, just as all the rafters of a peaked house lead to the roof peak*
> *and converge upon the roof peak, and all are removed when the roof*
> *peak is removed, so too all unwholesome states are rooted in ignorance*
> *and converge upon ignorance, and all are uprooted when ignorance*
> *is uprooted. Therefore, bhikkhus, you should train yourselves thus:*
> *"We will dwell diligently." Thus should you train yourselves.*
>
> (Saṃyutta Nikāya 20:1)

A person determined to better his or her situation in the universe will
"dwell diligently," striving to uproot ignorance by means of the Noble
Eightfold Path: right view, right intention, right speech, right action,
right livelihood, right effort, right mindfulness, and right concentration.
Because ignorance—specifically, ignorance about suffering, its origin,
its cessation, and the way to its cessation—is so crucial in the arising of
the sorrows of existence, we might assume that all troubles begin exactly
here, and that ignorance out of itself independently gives rise to the great
inertial sequences of life and death. But this is not correct. Ignorance is
indeed the fundamental defilement that supports craving and misleads
us endlessly, but ignorance is not the beginning of this dependently
arisen universe, and ignorance does not have a beginning itself in any
temporal sense. Like all other conditions, it does not stand alone and
unsupported. The Buddha explains:

> *A first beginning of ignorance cannot be conceived [of which it can*
> *be said]: "Before that, there was no ignorance and it came to be after*
> *that." Though this is so, monks, yet a specific condition of ignorance*
> *can be conceived. Ignorance, too, has its nutriment, I declare.... And*
> *what is the nutriment of ignorance? "The five hindrances" should be*
> *the answer.*
>
> (Aṅguttara Nikāya 10:61)

Although ignorance cannot be said to have had a beginning in time, it is nevertheless conditioned; it is supported, fed, renewed by the "nutriment" of the five hindrances: sensual desire, ill will, lethargy and drowsiness, agitation and worry, and doubt. These five tenacious factors afflict us to different degrees at different times, and meanwhile one cumulative effect they have is to promote and sustain ignorance. Yet we would be mistaken if we thought that here we have at last come to the beginning, the absolute origin of trouble and suffering, because the five hindrances themselves are conditioned phenomena that depend on other phenomena. The Buddha says that the hindrances have a nutriment, too, and that nutriment is "the three ways of wrong conduct"—misbehavior by body, speech, and thought.

Thus our search for definitive causes or beginnings leads us deeper; the roots of phenomena spread out disconcertingly. The three ways of wrong conduct have "lack of sense control" as their own nutriment. This lack of sense control is no independent thing, either; it in turn has as its own nutriment "lack of mindfulness and clear comprehension." By this point we should be realizing the hopelessness of tracking down any single, absolute starting point of the process of conditionality, for it appears more and more that phenomena are linked, related, and mutually conditioned. Indeed, the Buddha does not stop his explanation here but goes on to say that lack of mindfulness and clear comprehension has as its nutriment "careless attention." But is careless attention spontaneous, original, uncaused? Not at all. Its own nutriment is "lack of faith." And what is it that brings about lack of faith? "Listening to wrong teachings," says the Buddha. What then brings about this lamentable misfortune? What nourishes it and makes it possible? "Association with unworthy people," says the Buddha.

There are many ways by which we may fall into trouble. Errors in understanding and errors in action set off further errors and lead to the growth of harmful things. If we associate with unworthy, untrue, unreliable people, it is to be expected that we will hear wrong teachings. This will in turn contribute to lack of faith in what is good and true. Lack of faith makes it more likely that we will give careless attention to useless or harmful things. Careless attention then contributes to lack of mindfulness and clear comprehension. Without mindfulness, we are likely to lose control of our senses, to be overcome and deceived by the impressions that flash upon eye, ear, nose, tongue, body, and mind. Lack of sense control then serves as nutriment or stimulus for wrong conduct in our deeds, our words, and our thoughts; and wrong conduct promotes and fortifies the five hindrances, which again sustain the grievous defilement of ignorance.

So one mistake prepares the next, keeping ignorance dominant in the mind, with the result that birth and death and all the sorrows we know and fear go on whirling around without conclusion. This process of cause or nutriment can, however, work for our good if we pay heed to how phenomena influence one another. By associating as much as possible with virtuous persons, for example, we make it much more likely that we will hear true teachings and receive valuable advice. Then we have a basis for the development of faith, careful attention, and further wholesome factors that do not perpetuate ignorance but instead make possible enlightenment.

Although the doctrine of dependent origination is extremely profound, we can glean from the Buddha's summaries that although phenomena are brought about by countless interrelated factors over great spans of time, attention right now to wholesome principles of action will certainly increase our understanding, improve our fortune, and decrease our suffering. Death and rebirth are still mysteries to us, and we cannot instantly attain to a sovereign view, like the Buddha had, of beings wandering from life to life according to their deeds; but by listening to the Buddha's teachings and by observing what we can of action and result right here on the smaller scale of our own experience, we can gain the satisfactory faith that the way of Dhamma is a good and true way through this world and on to the next. The universe endlessly repeats itself, but wise actions will always bring good fruit and when fully purified will lead to liberation at last:

Again and again, they sow the seed;
Again and again, the sky-god sends down rain;
Again and again, plowmen plow the field;
Again and again, grain comes to the realm.

Again and again, the mendicants beg;
Again and again, the donors give;
When donors have given again and again,
Again and again they go to heaven.

Again and again, the dairy folk draw milk;
Again and again, the calf goes to its mother;
Again and again, one wearies and trembles;
Again and again, the dolt enters the womb;
Again and again, one is born and dies;
Again and again, they take one to the cemetery.

But when one has obtained the path
That leads to no more renewed existence,
Having become broad in wisdom,
One is not born again and again!

(Saṃyutta Nikāya 7:12)

What sort of birth, what sort of fortune awaits us, when this ardent, questioning life runs out? No one can tell us this. We must look to our actions. Do we exercise our bodies for good or evil? To what purpose do we speak? To what sort of thoughts do we return again and again? The universe has no care to caution us or encourage us; it just reflects, as it were, the actions we perform and forget. Those actions become our future. We must see to it that they are noble.

9. February in the Hills

HERE IS A PLEASANT SCENE: a small room with a fire snapping faintly against sooty bricks, a couple of worn armchairs, a table laden with books, and a big window overlooking wintry hollow and hill. The landscape is frosty and dramatic, and we, conscious of the steady warmth behind us, are standing here with arms comfortably folded, gazing at clouds and forest as the afternoon sun flashes over all.

What an odd, pinkish light it is that colors the outlines of clouds. We never see quite the same tinge in summer. It comes in mornings and late afternoons in cold weather like this, strangely counterfeiting warmth even as the wind does its freezing work on the landscape. The clouds are moving pretty swiftly, we can see, parting and combining and speeding supple shadows over ridges and lowlands. The forest that falls away beneath us is in motion, too, with treetops rocking in a way that suggests a kind of grace in the midst of what is otherwise the stolidity of winter. We are pleased to imagine (although in truth we cannot hear it) that the twigs and dry leaves vibrating in the wind together give out a grand, elemental music over all the country. Thus, with light and movement and music, nature *should* be displaying an underlying bounty and goodness despite the season, should it not? Ah, it should indeed! We agree with ourselves (there being nobody else to consult) and go on admiring the pinkish light in the clouds in the hope that we can soon believe the sky is not as cold as we suspect it is.

The snow that lies on the land is a meager effusion of late February that has none of the richness of deeper winter. Having melted and refrozen once or twice, it looks stark and shiny beneath the woods, reflecting back the sky's light and showing us the bulges and creases of the earth that we never see in the leafy summer. Our gaze slides down the slopes and the crooked lines of creeks all the way to the shadowed depths of the hollow and then wanders easily up to the top of the next ridge. Beyond, there are more ridges, vanishing at last into the harsh, wild sky. We are standing in a house high up in the wind and sunlight, with a rare view before us that should, we think, make us feel thoroughly glad. Rough as a winter might be out here amid forests and farms, this is not bad; and we are coming around to an attitude almost of exultation. Summer, winter, any season—how magnificent they are, how full of beauty! It emboldens us almost—but not quite—to declare life categorically good.

Light and color in the sky beyond the window glass, supplemented by warmth of furnace and fireplace in the house, give us a sensation that is aesthetically pleasing, certainly, but intellectually still a little troubling. We notice doubt in the middle of our comfortable reflections. It seems a pity that, although we try, we cannot just idle by the window and feel *entirely* satisfied. Such is the questioning nature of the mind that we must pick at these elements of our sensory experience and look for sources of the feelings that course through us. Is it not strange, for example, that we should approve a landscape that must seem to all other creatures today a desolation and a danger? Does the wind really sing, as we would have it, or does it jeer and menace, or does it merely hiss without meaning over the heads of creatures? That might depend on who is listening. The deer nibbling at the bark of saplings and the rabbits nosing through yellow grass have no time for abstractions like beauty; and the woodpeckers we glimpse stalking up and down big trees in the hollow are most likely just enduring, not exulting in any inedible glory of nature. How is it, then, that *we* can be connoisseurs of clouds and devotees of icy winds?

Situation, it would appear, has much to do with it. There is, above all, our favorable situation as human beings equipped with reason enough to comprehend or at least to reflect on things beyond the exigencies of the moment. The human mind must have something to chew on, and, given leisure, it will chew on beauty and find enjoyment if it can. Then, too, our particular situation today must greatly shape our attitude. We are fed, we are sheltered, and we philosophize with a fire behind us. We forget the fire, perhaps, but its warmth no doubt inclines us toward a complacent view of the snow beyond the window glass. Our own comfort adds more than a little to our appreciation of beauty generally and our willingness to see goodness in nature. If, instead of lounging in a warm room, we were hiking a long way overland, hatless and with wet shoes and thin coat, we might make of clouds, woods, and snow a different kind of picture.

We cannot regret our comfort this hour—we are very glad of it—but we begin to wonder how the situations, circumstances, and conditions that surround us might touch or even drive our philosophy. Do we really originate anything, or are these enthusiasms of ours just the predictable products of hunger and satiety, pain and pleasure, affliction and comfort? Would it not be good, for the sake of true knowledge, to be able to escape for a while the intellectual constriction of our environment?

We thought that a sojourn out here in solitude would free us from worry and let us be at peace with nature, but now we suspect that we are subtly cramped by the very pleasures we sought to help our meditation. Our view of the world outside us, to say nothing of our introspection, remains deeply subjective, too much tied to our own state of comfort to trust as absolutely true. We have had a fine lunch—and nature suddenly looks bountiful. We are warmed by a fire—and the red cedars in the wind become picturesque. We drowse in an armchair—and hills and sky radiate tranquility. After a nap we rise and stretch—and are pleased to discover a happy vigor in all of nature. How sound are these observations? The idea grows upon us that our sense of well-being as we scan the landscape is largely illusory and not likely to hold up under life's sharp changes.

We are situated this afternoon in a small house on a hilltop with lands and skies scenically disposed around us, but we still have not got enough of reality into our senses. How shall we climb up to a higher, more objective view? Or do we even want such a frightening power? We get, to be sure, a rare, ethereal pleasure from contemplating lonely landscapes, but possibly we are confusing that pleasure with insight.

A sudden pop from the fireplace interrupts our cogitations. The logs settle a little, and pop again. We can feel the heat pressing on our skin and smell the wood smoke. We hear a slight creaking from the window as the wind pushes at it. A pause of quiet watchfulness reveals a myriad of sensations darting through our limbs. There is, as there has always been, a multiplicity of small things happening—a flow, a flood, a cataract of events whose meaning we almost always construe subjectively, according to the pleasure or displeasure they arouse in us. In regard both to our bodies and to house and hilltop and visible landscape, our understanding is held down by the weight of personal interest. If the weather is lovely, very well, it is lovely to *us* but not, fairly speaking, to all conscious creatures. If it is harsh, that is how *we* receive it, but we have not thereby attained to any comprehensive view. Would it be possible, though, to desist from dreaming and to establish mindfulness so firmly that things would appear to us in their plain nature—would arise and pass away uncontaminated by conceit?

This is a mystery we still have barely glimpsed: the idea of dwelling in unadorned reality, of perceiving the plainness of things in themselves. It is very doubtful that we could expect pleasure alone from such a vision. We are eager, certainly, to be reassured that all the universe, if looked at rightly, is a perennial garden of perfection, and that this winter, too, (screened off discreetly by window glass) blooms with its own species of loveliness. But when we lay aside our comfortable situation and discount as far as possible the lunch we consumed, we sense the inadequacy of such a view. The snowy lawn just below us bears streaks and scratches—the tracks of small creatures—and these remind us that we have not yet seen from the level of the snow, have not sufficiently considered the various fates of beings. How could we summarize the world as good when we speak only for ourselves and only for a moment?

The pinkish clouds and the bold blue sky are scenic—and we would not wish for sleet instead—but still, as changing things, they change and cannot serve our pleasure very long. Besides, we are not at all impartial in our observations; we are not comprehensive: we turn toward what we like and find those things significant, while what bores us or disgusts us simply recedes and vanishes. A young green pine on the hillside, for instance, attracts our contemplation, and we are happy to admire it; but does it better represent the state of the universe than the drab, dead moss on the boulder underneath it? We let taste, preference, and partiality have more to do with our philosophy and our apprehension of truth than we would gladly recognize.

This failing—for it is just that—is why we ought to meditate, why we ought to step back from the sensory tumult and watch it cautiously. We need a more comprehensive and dispassionate view. Meditation should not be any kind of indulgence in the agreeable moment, not a striving to make the world hold still, not a haranguing of ourselves to *feel serene.* Rather it should be an effort to set up mindfulness and see phenomena for what they are in their raw nature. It may be that we have already more or less decided what we will discover about the hidden features of reality. That is an error, because we are thus presupposing truths without foundation and implicitly assuming that mere self-interest can determine reality. What kind of honorable life can stand on a fantasy, however sentimental, attractive, and reassuring? If we say the world is good and glorious, we must rigorously ignore or tortuously reinterpret too many scenes of pain, too many cries of suffering beings, too many piteous deaths and bereavements. Meditation, rightly practiced, should be a brave and concentrated look into just what is.

The green pine tree shall have its place, but so shall the dead stalks of last year's lilies. The blue, blown heavens deserve our contemplation, but so does the wretched shed over there in a field, rotting away under heavy vines, and so do the cast-off pieces of farm machinery rusting into strange symbols in ditches and thickets. Meditation must take account of decay as well as growth, not assuming the supremacy of either but considering both from a fair, judicious stance. Are we warm and rested and do we rejoice in February's severe beauty? Very good. But not all beings do. Can we simply acknowledge our personal satisfactions and move on to see, as far as imagination can, through the eye of the crow that sways on a high oak bough or the eye of the squirrel that skitters across the snow?

We have come out to the country to think and be free, but maybe we esteem freedom in too crude a sense—as freedom to indulge our desires, freedom to follow the dictates of craving, freedom to pretend and presume without contradiction. What about the freedom to know without the encumbrance of conceit? Instead of staying bound to one pitiful, mortal, absurdly subjective viewpoint, squeezed by the interests of a tyrannical "I," what if we could get loose and be silent and merely watch?

The fire crackles and ticks and whistles as the afternoon wears away and our own thinking wears away. Shall we read for a while? All right, there goes another hour in patterns of ideas and images, whence we emerge entertained though not, it seems, appreciably wiser. Shall we take a cloth to the smudges on the window now lit up by the low sun? Good, that is done, and no great fears or delights have assailed us. Now it is time to shove a couple of logs into the fireplace, fiddle with the firescreen, and admire the sparks rushing up the chimney. It is likely it will get colder tonight, so we will need more firewood—not entirely for the heat, because the furnace is doing its job, but for our amusement, maybe, or our consolation. We look at the door, a little reluctantly, suspecting that the weather has not got any more hospitable now that the sun is going down through heavy clouds crowding in from the west.

But we cannot mope and doze within these walls forever. Let's hurry out at least so we can say we have not neglected the experience of winter. All right, here is the door clattering open. Now then, what is outside? Ah, what brilliant light, even so late in the day, almost painful. What icy air curls around us! Huffing a little more dramatically than we really need to, we go plodding a short way across the yard to the woodpile, our shoes driving noisily into the snow. We would have been wiser to put on some boots, no doubt. When we pull back the plastic tarpaulin and lay our gloved hands on the logs and then pause a moment, we can hear at last the wind we have been imagining; but it is dying away now with the day—just faintly troubling the branches of a red cedar above us. The sky, we notice regretfully, is swiftly losing its exalted blue.

Out here our view is wider than ever, extending on one side over miles of ridges and valleys (now going dim in their depths) to the murky, unspectacular redness of the western horizon. On the other side, we are closed in by fields running up to scraggly woods; and we are aware of a ridiculous disappointment that we cannot look out that way, too, as far away into infinity as we would like. As we struggle to gather up the cold, split pieces of oak, our grunts and gasps and the clunking and scraping of the wood strangely emphasize the deepening silence and solemnity around us.

By the time we are headed back to the house with an unwieldy load of logs in our arms, we have entirely lost any sentiments of exaltation and sunny satisfaction. Here is the door again; we bumble through it into the warm house and dump the wood, with startling crashes, into the iron rack by the fireplace. Good, but not enough. Out we go again, puffing industriously as if to distract ourselves from the winter's gravity. We hop across the yard, more or less landing in our previous footprints but still getting a quantity of snow into our shoes before we reach the wood-pile. Our ears sting with the cold, and we do not stand very long admiring hills and hollows and darkening heavens. They are there as background immensities as we, very small and shivery, pick at the heavy logs and try not to mash our fingers. Ah, three or four good-sized pieces—is this enough to carry? With our splintery burden imperfectly balanced, we go slipping and staggering back to the porch, and up the steps without trouble, and again into the surprising heat and closeness of the house.

How much wood will suffice for the night, or anyway for the hours we intend to stay awake? We have no idea. And how much wood or fuel or entertainment (it now oddly occurs to us) will we require for our peace of mind throughout this whole hungry life? Could we ever calculate or acquire such a provision? Oh, at any rate, let us get a couple more logs.

On our third trip back from the woodpile, growing a little embarrassed at our timorous haste, we force ourselves to stop for a moment. Shall we not just stand right here and take a breath, cold though it be, and try to get some honest feeling for the dusk, for the great, bleak sphere of earth and space in which we briefly live? Shall we hold on here just a little? All right—one breath, two, three, and a few more uncounted and unbegrudged. We are better aware, now that we try, of the blurring sky with its purple and red, and the woods going dark, and the disheveled fields without birds and silent, and the flat open snow shining blankly around us. We are aware of the tension in our muscles and the heat of blood moving in our limbs and the aching cold of snow around our ankles. Loneliness, wonder, strange fear, and even peace pass through us without words.

We turn slowly, as if to single out a worthy impression to carry away—a token of the vanishing moment. Shall it be an oak branch pleasingly displayed against the sky? Or a crimson reflection in a window pane? Or maybe here, close by the southern side of the house—yes, some blunt green shoots of daffodils just starting up through half-frozen mud. It is the end of February, after all, and these are not the first new plants appearing in these parts, so we are not surprised or especially inspired. But if we were about to sink gloomily under an apprehension of eternal winter, these daffodils are a contradiction to the snow that is worth observing. All formations change. For our caution, for our hope, this is good to know.

Our armload of wood is getting heavy, so we turn away and plod back around the house to the door. The cold is not really so terrible. With the days now swiftly lengthening, the process of spring is already underway despite the snow; and if we wished we might regard even the stark sky and the whole tremendous landscape as the merest phantoms flying past us, to be succeeded in scarcely a breath or two by other phantoms of nature, on around to the next fall and the next winter and beyond. All these go by in a flaring of sensations—why should we get upset by any?

Back in the house again, sniffling, dumping the logs, brushing off our clothes, stamping around to warm our feet, we manage to carry on, for a little while, the sensation of life passing comfortably. It is satisfying, anyway, to stack a couple of oak logs onto the coals in the fireplace and poke at them heartily until we have got the fire sparking and crackling loud. It is satisfying to sweep the hearth and otherwise clatter around with a broom, bumping the furniture, maybe cleaning and maybe just making noise. In the midst of our busyness we notice one motion melting into the next, one pattern of vision giving way to something else, one thought supplanted by another. It is not painful; it is rather interesting and refreshing. We find that with a little effort we can stand back from the small domestic flurry and see it happening before us as just a succession of impersonal events—not much different, really, from the gigantic progress of seasons out there in the hills. When we slacken in this mental effort, however, as happens soon enough, we become again conscious of a tedious, whining sense of personhood—and once more we are worrying how we shall stay amused or distracted through all this long evening ahead.

With the room clean and with no other obvious chores offering themselves, and with the doors and windows snugly closed and a lamp lighted beside our chair, we are prepared, we hope, to appreciate the evening in some spiritual sense, to read a book with real concentration, to meditate, or maybe just to stare peacefully out at snow and forest under moonlight. But tonight, as it turns out, there is no moonlight. We discover in a little while, when all effects of sunset (more phantoms yet) have died away, that this night will serve us no fine, sharp-focused stars and lyrical moon, no prospects of frosty, mystical hills and dreamy distance. We are closed in, muffled by dull, cold clouds, and we peer out over forested darkness in which we can find only a few lights of houses, far apart, at uncertain elevations and distances. The snow shows up a little in the hollow and on top of the nearest ridge, but the forms upon it we admired in the last hour have all become indistinct.

Looking out, we are moved to sigh (and how many million other beings sigh tonight, gazing over snow in their mortal solitude?). We are still waiting, hopeful and gloomy by turns, for nature to speak definitively and resolve all doubts. Such is our inertia. We complain of ignorance but keep on waiting, with no encouragement from the cycling seasons, to be informed, edified, and enlightened according to *our* notions. We flatter ourselves that we are sensitive and philosophical, but probably we do not mean to go much out of our way, if we can help it, to attain enlightenment. It would be much more agreeable if enlightenment would come to us, simply because of our luxurious longing.

Considering this disappointing, dreary night, however, considering the lifeless slush out there re-freezing in silence, considering the multitudes of creatures sleeping cold under piles of leaves or curled in damp holes in trees or roaming hungrily through the deep, silent hours, we cannot believe that the universe is arranged for pleasure or that desire alone can ever culminate in liberation. All beings desire; all ardently pursue their private interests—what is there in that? How many dispassionately pursue truth?

If we would really know truth, we must work—and not only at those tasks that immediately appeal to us. Intuition will urge us on a little way but will not hold us to a single course. When we drift among our whims and wishes we *have* no course; we wander more crookedly than any mouse across the snow. To secure our own welfare we surely need to set ourselves to a good path not of our own devising and follow it faithfully.

What path, then, deserves our trust? Gazing over the dark hills, for a moment forgetting our multitude of wants, we think of the Dhamma, and think of it now not just as so many doctrines listed in a book or so many traditions of religious observance or so many stories awaiting our casual attention, but rather as ageless truth, as an abiding reality as monumental as the stony hills, as a path that does not bend according to anybody's desire but goes on straight to the end of suffering. It might be that even while we have tried to understand and practice the Dhamma, we have still regarded it as a philosophy to sample and adapt, as a set of theories to fit into our still unaltered way of living. This cannot be right, cannot be wise. Is it not just more subservience to craving? What if, instead, by means of Dhamma, we sought to master that very craving?

In youth we imagined ourselves as explorers and adventurers, undertaking noble trials and winning through at last heroically, and even though the time and chance for such heroism never seemed to come, we still remember that near exaltation, that gathering energy that sought direction. Even now, though wearied and chastened by life's reverses, we sometimes feel a longing to escape the ordinary, to fight off resignation, to achieve and triumph. But how should we accomplish that? Whichever of our multitudinous wishes we light on in such moments appears a little shopworn and banal. Which of the usual bunch would we have—wealth, romance, adventure, power, fame, scientific discovery, artistic magnificence? These are all mundane goals, reachable, maybe, if we have the notion. We might call them worthwhile, one or another, now and then; but their gratifications are not rare in the world, not lasting, and also, if we reflect most carefully, not quite the answer to our longing.

In religion and philosophy, as in all things, we have long tried to satisfy unquestioned craving within ourselves; we have looked for reassurance—not so much for truth. But the Buddha, as we may now be discovering, proposes the radical overthrow of craving itself. He points, past all impermanent distractions, to the utter cessation of suffering and the attainment of perfect happiness; and that double and indeed identical goal can be achieved only when one abandons vanity and devotes oneself to the Noble Eightfold Path. As long as we insist on the primacy of our desires and opinions, as long as we try to revise truth in line with our liking, we can expect to remain sad, unsatisfied, and lost. Longing and strength of a sort we may possess for a vain year or two, but their consequence will be only more desperate wandering over the snow. Seen from a distance, our footprints will be broken and irregular, straying here and there and round about forever like the tracks of the rabbits and the mice.

But if we were to live by Dhamma without qualification, without subservience to conceit, we might discover at last our natural direction across the landscape of time. We might also find a channel for that inspiration of youth that still visits us when we gaze over the hills in February. We hope—and rightly hope—not to sink into resignation as age slowly chills us, but to get up and reach for what is higher and worthier than any earthly prize. This, indeed, is the bracing imperative that runs throughout the pages of the ancient Pāli Canon in the words of the Buddha, in stories of seekers and sages, and in verses that extol the majesty of striving. Here on this human plane there are the numberless joys of the senses, but there is also the rarer, finer joy of spiritual discovery and attainment. Heroism in the noblest sense is always possible, and that is what the Buddha urges upon us. To spurn what is base, to renounce what defiles, to pass by both what is beautiful and what is hideous without faltering, to do good, to seek for insight, to trust to a noble ideal across years or lifetimes—that is religion, and that is our preservation in the winter of ignorance.

Outside the window now such darkness prevails that in a while we realize we are seeing less of that external landscape than of the reflection

of this room, with the lamp, the fire, the furniture, and the ghostly form
we take to be our own. How strange, how metaphorical. Is this our true
substance after all? If it is, it does not seem to be a problem now. Maybe
our gaze is becoming a little less narrow. We look through our own
reflection onto a hillside that falls away into the wilderness of saṃsāra,
where beings without number wander and suffer and forget and wander
still. Some, though, we are coming to believe, undertake to live by
Dhamma, simply inspired and willing to act on inspiration. Some rise
out of the immemorial darkness, remembering the boldness of youth,
and do what they can with faith and honor.

The boundless night surrounds us, as it always has; but we are pleased
to contemplate out there those lone lights of houses, pleased to see them
as symbols of the good Dhamma still shining in the world. We remember, in our mortal frailty, that the Buddha once taught beings such as us,
knowing that the human mind could respond to the Dhamma; and we
wonder whether, come the cold daylight, we will be answering the message rightly.

Now there is a noise from somewhere—a thump, a scratching, something strange. Alarmed, we listen. The fire whispers and crackles. That
was not it. Some animal on the porch? Should we take a look? We move
to the door, not very speedily, and nervously crack it open. Cold air and
darkness pour silently over us—the universe is reduced to only that as
we stand blinking and faintly breathing. Wait, here is the switch for the
porch light. All right, now as we open the door wider we can see the icy
steps and a dim stretch of snow vanishing into eternity, and a strange,
gray shape wobbling slowly away from us.

What is it? We experience a moment of blank suspension, conscious
only of forms and darkness, and then the shape pauses and turns, and we
recognize it. An opossum! We are startled, then relieved and even glad-
dened. Ah, we have company in the wilderness, a fellow creature dropping by! Raising a hand, we are about to call out a jocular greeting—but
the words fade out at our lips as the ragged, furry shape edges around
sideways and stops and looks directly back at us.

Those eyes are bleak and loveless. They speak no intelligible greeting.
They stare at us intensely across the snow, only some yards away but in

another sense terrifically remote. Is it curiosity or fear or enmity that works in the opossum's mind as it pauses there, body balanced, head lifted, in the freezing night? What does it see when it looks at us? We cannot imagine. Wait, now—we *can* imagine. As in a window's reflection we see ourselves framed in the lit doorway—gawky, shivering, peering timorously out into the universe. How frail we are, we who can barely stand to step outdoors where the opossum dwells all through the year.

The opossum, without any expression that we can read, stares at us, unmoving, for another frigid minute. It will not be patronized by us; it will not be whistled into friendliness. It goes on by instinct, suffering and enduring with a strength that even we clever, fortunate beings might envy. But to be strong *and* to contemplate—that would be a better way of living. To see, undeludedly, the harshness of existence and yet stay kindly and composed—that surely is a state to reach for.

Without hurry, without further notice of us, the opossum turns its head away, stretches out a slow foot, and creeps away toward the line of the woods, becoming shadowy, abstract, and finally gone. For once, no words, no ideas occur to us. We listen and hear nothing, as the night flows cold over our limbs. The snow in the dim light near the steps is full of tracks turning here and there and round about forever. Slowly we step back and slowly we close the door. It is time to sleep.

But nature is always piling its incidents upon our unreadiness. Hardly have we covered ourselves in blankets and turned a last, marveling gaze toward the window, when it is morning again. The fire is dead, and the room is brightening with natural light, and we are planting our feet on the cold floor and getting up into the whirl of saṃsāra once again. Now then, where were we meaning to go? Shall it be a day to honor the Dhamma?

Outside, the sky is breaking apart in ribbons of blue and white. There is a wild pinkish tinge, too, to the clouds that are passing overhead. February is in the hills, but it is passing by as well. In a minute we are going to go outside and around to the southern side of the house to see how the shoots of the daffodils are doing.

10. Desperation and Peace

WHENEVER WE TAKE UP the excellent idea of reforming our lives in a full, spiritual sense, of seriously pursuing Buddhist ideals of virtue, concentration, and wisdom, we may find the work hampered not only by our own, very familiar, internal weaknesses but also in some respects by our social environment. We are susceptible to influences, and we get plenty of influences from the great churning and stewing of popular theory, enthusiasm, experiment, and custom all around us. We take note of—we even copy—what our friends do, what our colleagues do, and what seem to be the standards of the groups we belong to or aspire to join. Lamentably, these influences can sometimes be quite harmful when they appeal to and reinforce, with the multiplied strength of general approval, our own unwise tendencies.

One of the most cherished—and by now practically unassailable—beliefs of most of contemporary society is that sexual desire is naturally good, beautiful, beneficial, and deserving of the fullest possible expression. Love, as a more spiritual sort of affection, is generally admitted as an advantageous accompaniment, along with a degree of respect for others and an awareness of possible hazards; but no qualification much dims the central, popular conviction that sexuality is and must be one of the highest adornments and purposes of human life, to be indulged in with fervor and without shame. Thus youth and beauty, being the supreme focus of sexual desire, are extravagantly adored in our society; the flame of passion is passionately fanned (lest it should, unthinkably, go out);

and all around, by provocative images and words, the ideal of sensual pleasure is polished to a dazzling brightness.

It would seem that an age of sophisticated, guiltless joy should have come about by now, but we know, alas, that it has not. We have our own quiet doubts and disillusionments, and perhaps we notice that in the lives of others the universally extolled sexual liberty seems strangely related to trouble and, indeed, misery. Is this a trivial coincidence? We try to will ourselves to confidence, to bathe in the brilliance of modern views, but still we lapse into unexplained sadness; still shadows loom over us and rebellious questions break out. Who can answer them? Getting a little tired, perhaps, of the manic worship of sex and beginning to mistrust even our own powerful instincts, we would like to know what to do and what not to do and—most important—why that should be so. We had escaped from guilt, we thought, into all this delirious freedom of sexual expression; but now, after much fear, blundering, and regret, we find ourselves still brooding over the right and the wrong and the deeper questions about the meaning of our passions. If, as it seems, sexual desire is neither going to disappear from our minds any time soon nor lead infallibly to happiness, how exactly shall we deal with it?

Early in any investigation of Buddhist teaching we come across the five basic moral precepts for lay people: to abstain from killing, from stealing, from sexual misconduct, from telling lies, and from taking intoxicants. Sexual misconduct (literally "misconduct in sensual pleasures") refers to adultery and all other illicit, coercive, and abusive kinds of sexual behavior; that is, having sexual relations with the wives or husbands of others, or with engaged persons, or with children, or with anyone unwilling or helpless, or with any other persons protected by law or custom. All such actions are bad and reprehensible and not to be done.

But why? This precept sounds at first just like a set of prohibitions—which we may or may not find reasonable. Why should we observe this precept or any religious rules about sexual behavior? The norms of contemporary society, such as they are, are less specific and more elastic—which is certainly convenient—and even if we would in theory accept rules of some kind, why shouldn't we just make them up for ourselves or admit only those in Buddhism that unequivocally appeal to us? Since we, like everyone else, do not care for restriction of any sort, why shouldn't we just improvise according to changing circumstances and our own insights—assuming we can learn to organize the latter a little better than we do now? Don't rules cramp our freedom? And shouldn't freedom be preserved and enlarged at all costs?

Buddhism contains definite, specific doctrines of behavior concerning sexuality and all aspects of life, and it also contains explanations, reasons, and illustrations that show why certain things should or should not be done. The *why* of its moral teachings is important not only for intellectual satisfaction but also for the faith and the healthy energy it arouses in one who seeks a noble happiness. So beyond just glancing over lists of precepts, we ought to read a little deeper into the wise principles beneath them. One of the characteristics of the Dhamma, often mentioned in the Pāli Canon, is that it is "inviting"—it is entirely open to study. If we want to know the *why* of any moral standard, we can find out.

To begin with, the lay Buddhist precept on sexual misconduct is, like the other four precepts, not a rule in the ordinary sense. It is not a prohibition imposed on us by the Buddha or any individual or institution that has authority over us. It is not an order, an injunction, a laid-down law. Rather it is a guideline that we take upon ourselves voluntarily, that we determine to follow for our own good, in order to avoid suffering and obtain happiness. This is a very important point. When the Buddha explains this and the other precepts he is explaining the right way—the wise way—to deal with certain processes that operate in the universe quite independently of human desires; he is pointing out how those processes may bring suffering or happiness according to the choices we make and the courses of action we follow. If we do certain kinds of actions, certain corresponding results naturally tend to arise for us. If we intentionally kill or steal or commit sexual misconduct or tell lies, we will set going dismal processes that produce suffering for us as a matter of course. If we intoxicate ourselves with liquor or drugs, we will lose our sense of caution and our resistance to destructive passions. This is the basic *why* behind the precepts. Whether understood or not, whether approved of or not, causes accumulate and produce appropriate results.

When the Buddha warns his followers not to engage in some kind of behavior, it is not because he wants to stop them from enjoying themselves but because he understands the underlying process of causality in that behavior that leads to suffering. A person who respects and observes the moral precepts that the Buddha teaches is carrying out a sensible program of honorable self-restraint that does not produce suffering and that by its nature leads instead to increasing well-being, both for himself and for the society around him.

In the matter of sexual desire, adherence to specific standards is essential, because feeble guidelines of our own devising are easily obliterated by lust. Moral improvising misleads us into deeper confusion and sorrow. When we experience strong desire and do not recognize absolute limits to our behavior, there will be a powerful tendency to justify that desire and let it carry us along. If we are tempted toward unfaithfulness and adultery, for example, we might think that, although we disapprove of such behavior in the abstract, our own case is strikingly unique and eminently excusable. But everybody thinks his own case unique and excusable and supposes that all bad consequences should be suspended for his sake. It is doubtful that the laws of the universe are much affected.

We might also attempt to argue that, whatever the morality of a situation might technically be, *love* justifies—love makes it good. But this is frightfully wrong. Love, or what is called love, does nothing of the sort—it only urges. It is the function of wisdom to restrain the urge when it is bad. Neither love nor any other powerful desire can prevent bad actions from producing fitting results.

We might even understand, in theory, the law of kamma, of intentional action and its results, but it is still easy to compromise and surrender to sexual desire even in clearly reprehensible circumstances. Giving in is agreeable; it seems very natural; and, especially nowadays, it is seldom much frowned upon by society. To oppose this desire, on the other hand, seems arduous, lonely, and counter to our instinct. Thus the moral argument in our minds might not be very serious: lacking the aid of Dhamma, we might timidly advance a doubt about some contemplated action and then let it be blasted away by the sheer heat of desire. Oh, we must be free! We must express our beautiful passion! So we tell ourselves. We are already giving in, already pursuing some fatal course, while our cowed reason feebly consents. It scarcely matters—it is really just a question of form to keep the conscience silent.

But if we insist on our prerogative to do whatever we *want,* we are in actual effect insisting on miserable servitude for ourselves, because to answer obediently all the commands of desire can be nothing other than servitude, made all the more oppressive by ignorance of what is really going on. We are compelled, driven, haunted, kept jumping by internal passions we do not comprehend. We scramble here and there after pleasure in the pitiful belief that this is freedom.

From a Buddhist point of view freedom is the ability to act autonomously and independently out of wisdom, not out of instinct. What wisdom makes clear is that, regardless of hopes and opinions, actions still have palpable consequences, and there are certain principles of action that, if followed, naturally lead to peace and safety. These the wise person honors and follows.

Faced with the fury of our own instinct and enveloped in the hedonism of contemporary society, we need the help of the explicit precepts taught by the Buddha. These trustworthy standards do not compromise our freedom at all; rather they protect us from the terrible and often unrecognized tyranny of craving. They serve us especially in those times when we are powerfully tempted and cannot reason with much steadiness or strength. It is perfectly right that we should resolve to be, in matters of love and sex and everything else, faithful, self-controlled, and honorable; but in the absence of real understanding and conviction those qualities remain subjective, indefinite, vague, and thus not meaningful in practice. What are faith, self-control, and honor—beyond high-sounding words? Do we know, or are we guessing and revising definitions just to suit our desires of the moment? To attain any moral safety we must stand upon specifics, and we find reliable specifics in the five precepts, which have behind them the wisdom of the Buddha and the weight of twenty-five hundred years of Buddhist tradition.

The Buddha shows by his teaching that he is perfectly aware of human weaknesses and is nevertheless intent on helping all who sincerely want to improve themselves. The five moral precepts for lay followers, including the precept on sexual misconduct, are not burdens, not hindrances to freedom of action at all, but mild and sensible guidelines for social peace and spiritual liberation. Lay people are not expected to observe celibacy as do the monks and nuns but simply to behave with modesty, self-restraint, kindness, and decorum, recognizing decent, spelled-out limits. To keep within these limits—never engaging in adultery, never having sexual relations with under-age or otherwise unsuitable persons—is to discipline oneself morally and to advance spiritually. Such wise self-governance protects families, ensures peace and self-respect, and strengthens the individual against the world's uncertainties.

The Buddha does not (as much of the world seems inclined to do) regard sexual passion as specially entitled to indulgence on account of its fiery, urgent nature. He teaches the control of all passions as a foundation for security, a basis for worldly happiness, and an essential aspect of the training for enlightenment. There must be, to begin with, control of body and speech—morality in the basic sense—and this is what the five precepts are principally concerned with. When body and speech are controlled it becomes possible to govern the subtler and swifter actions of the mind and thus gradually to reduce one's liability to error and suffering.

When there is no effort at control, however, unwholesome causes will multiply and brew disasters, irrespective of one's opinions or the fashions of any age. When sexual desire is taken as the unquestionable determinant of one's actions, and when sexual indulgence is deemed the worthiest possible experience, considerations of good sense and honor fade from the mind. Kindness fades, too—for who can be kind, who can show disinterested benevolence, when the sovereign imperative is immediately to please oneself? There is no dignity, no stature, certainly no nobility in life given over to burning instinct.

The result of unrestrained lust, no matter how generally condoned or admired, is not happiness, not fulfillment, but wretchedness and despair. "Lust," to be sure, is a grim old word not much fancied nowadays, not much used except in a joking, uneasy way, because it connotes unseemly desire, something ugly, offensive, and ignoble; but a clear description requires clear terminology. Contemporary society, it would seem, is anxious to obscure the ugly side of sexuality, believing that the sexual impulse needs, if anything, greater liberty in order to produce the strangely delayed happiness and fulfillment. The Pāli scriptures, on the other hand, speak very bluntly about lust and its dangers. "Lust" *(rāga)* and "greed" *(lobhā)* are there used frequently and almost synonymously. All kinds of lust and greed are defilements, and from defilements much misery can be expected in the long run.

From basic Buddhist doctrine it follows that those influences in the world that tend to provoke lust and greed ought to be avoided. Such provocation is, as it happens, one of those things that human beings do not profit from at all and can comfortably live without. We all have plenty of desires as it is, and there can be no purpose in provoking them except to accelerate a pursuit that is already desperate and exhausting. Salacious entertainment, pornography, lascivious banter, and all other kinds of sexual crudeness, however common or nominally accepted in society, should be avoided both because they degrade social life and because they wreck our own internal balance and bring sharp suffering upon us.

Besides abstaining from vulgarity, it is very much worthwhile to develop a positive, countervailing power: the lovely, often-forgotten quality of modesty. The sexual side of human life gets ample attention already—nobody is going to forget it—and there can be no advantage, and certainly no charm, in grossly dwelling on it in our words and manners. Modesty is not only a tactful reticence on sexual subjects but also an attitude of strength and dignity. Harping on physical beauty and sexual pleasure in this ever-aging, suffering universe betrays pitiful ignorance and unseemly craving. The modest person declines to display himself or herself in unseemly ways and, mindful of the sensibilities of other people, behaves instead with tact and consideration, refraining from obscene language and offensive familiarity. Over time, self-control and composure earn esteem.

As we progress in our study of the Dhamma, we should begin to notice that the brutality and moral ugliness in society and in individual behavior proceed from untreated defilements in the mind and, being indulged in, worsen those same defilements. We practice the Dhamma not to reconcile ourselves to our defilements but to rid ourselves of them. On one occasion recorded in the Pāli Canon, Venerable Sāriputta, one of the

Buddha's two chief disciples, tells the monks that if, when they wander abroad, wise people should ask them what their teacher teaches, they should answer in this way: "Our teacher, friends, teaches the removal of desire and lust." If questioned further, they should explain, "Our teacher, friends, teaches the removal of desire and lust for form, the removal of desire and lust for feeling...for perception...for mental formations...for consciousness." If they are then asked what benefit their teacher sees in this course they should answer thus:

> *If, friends, one is devoid of lust, desire, affection, thirst, passion, and craving in regard to form...feeling...perception...mental formations...consciousness, then with the change and alteration of form...feeling...perception...mental formations...with the change and alteration of consciousness sorrow, lamentation, pain, dejection, and despair do not arise in one.*
>
> (Saṃyutta Nikāya 22:2)

The material form, feeling, perception, mental formations, and consciousness that make up all desired and undesired persons are at bottom mere aggregates *(khandhas)*—groups of unsubstantial processes. These aggregates, moreover, inevitably undergo "change and alteration," and that solemn fact is what makes lustful hopes go awry and end in suffering. When, however, one removes lust, the suffering cannot come to be, even though the world and all its parts go on changing. When the cause is lacking, the effect does not occur.

What this means in the ordinary experience of ordinary people can be seen in an illustration that the Buddha gives:

> *Suppose, bhikkhus, a man loved a woman with his mind bound to her by intense desire and passion. He might see that woman standing with another man, chatting, joking, and laughing. What do you think, bhikkhus? Would not sorrow, lamentation, pain, dejection, and despair arise in that man when he sees that woman standing with another man, chatting, joking, and laughing?*
>
> (Majjhima Nikāya 101:24)

Here begins, we can see, another of a thousand tales of grief. Conflict is already gathering. But it need not go on as we expect. That man, the Buddha says, might think, "What if I were to abandon my desire and lust for that woman?" Then, it might be, he does just that, so that at a later time when he sees that same woman talking with another man, no misery arises in him. The sorrow, lamentation, pain, dejection, and despair of the hapless lover depend upon his own desire and lust. Let that jealous man restrain and dispel the desire and lust, and then, no matter who talks with whom, he has no cause for sorrow and abides at peace.

If we have never learned the wisdom of self-restraint, or have never become convinced of the beneficent truths of the Dhamma, we will likely assume that desire and lust, being so compelling, so intoxicating, and so nearly overwhelming, must be obeyed by all means and that external circumstances in all their wild complexity must, by whatever struggles, be arranged according to our hopes. Then, sadly, as circumstances irresistibly change and do not work out pleasantly, there will follow jealousy, bitterness, and many other forms of misery on down to despair, owing to the uncontrollable nature of others' affections and the variability of the universe at large. Such desperate dependence and helplessness hardly seem wise.

The Buddha, meanwhile, calmly points to the process of cause and effect beneath this immemorial problem. Those persons whom we desire have their own whims and are driven by their own inscrutable passions, which we try desperately to control but cannot. We supply, with our single-minded craving, the essential cause for our own suffering. But let that cause be removed, let the unreasoning passion be restrained, and no agonies of disappointment follow; no woeful stories of rivalry and grief need be told.

Sexual pleasures, no matter how intense, have the same flaw as all pleasures of the senses: they are impermanent, unsubstantial, and quickly fading. But the impulsive desire for such pleasures, being so intoxicating, so fiery, can rout quieter intentions of self-control and decency and draw the unwary into reckless, destructive actions—all sorts of cruelty, faithlessness, and selfishness—which may not, indeed, seem bad at first but which nevertheless bring after them misfortune, bitterness, and remorse. We surely have no wish to endure what so many others endure through their heedlessness, and yet, as we gaze around at the alluring images of lust and gratification that swirl through contemporary society, and as we consider their implicit promises of delight and guiltless satisfaction, perhaps we are not entirely unattracted. Knowing ourselves as subject to sensual desires, we might wonder whether the Dhamma only offers us a defense against blame and misery (which we might admit is a good thing) or whether it could also give us some kind of superior joy or peace.

Here it is encouraging to remember that the Buddha declares that he teaches for the "welfare and happiness" of living beings. There is definitely happiness obtainable in this life and in future lives through consistent generosity, integrity, and self-restraint. With no bad conscience, with no remorse over shameful deeds, one lives lightly, free from fear. And above all there is Nibbāna, the supreme joy toward which the Noble Eightfold Path reliably leads. Nibbāna is at once the complete escape from suffering and the highest possible happiness. There really is no distinction—it just depends on how we wish to look at it.

In those restful and perhaps rare moments when no fierce desire possesses us, when we calmly recall some good deed we have done or simply let ideas and impressions come and go peacefully without clinging to any of them, we get a fine presentiment of great joys yet to come that have nothing to do with fever and fear. Maybe we have too long thought of happiness as a procession of ever-intensifying pleasures. What about simply letting go of things that defile us and torment us?

In the Pāli Canon we find recorded a beautiful incident in the life of the Buddha that illustrates this way of looking at happiness. Prince Hatthaka of Ālavi, out one day wandering for exercise in the forest, comes upon the Buddha sitting on a spread of leaves on a cattle path. It is the cold season, but there is the Buddha sitting on the ground, protected only by his thin robes. Hatthaka salutes him respectfully and sits down nearby. No doubt perplexed, he asks politely whether the Buddha has slept well. The Buddha answers, "Yes, prince, I have slept well." Then Hatthaka expresses his surprise:

*Venerable sir, the winter nights are cold, and this is a week when
there is frost. Hard is the ground trampled by the hooves of cattle, thin
is the spread of leaves, sparse are the leaves on the trees, thin are the
tawny robes, and cold blows the Verambha wind. Yet the Blessed
One says, "Yes, prince, I have slept well...."*

The Buddha then poses a question for Hatthaka. Suppose there was
"a householder or householder's son" living in a house with a gabled
roof, plastered and protected against wind, with all doors and windows
closed. And suppose in this house, thus made comfortable, there was a
couch with scarlet cushions and luxurious covers. And suppose there
was a lamp burning there, and this man had four wives to wait on him.
In such circumstances, would he sleep well? When Hatthaka says, yes,
he would, the Buddha asks him to consider a further possibility:

*What do you think, prince? Might there not arise in that householder
or householder's son vexations of body or mind, caused by lust, so
that, tormented by them, he might sleep badly?*

When Hatthaka agrees that this could happen, the Buddha points to
a striking truth:

*Now, prince, the lust by which that householder or householder's son
is tormented and which causes him to sleep badly, that lust, prince,
has been abandoned by the Tathāgata, cut off at the root, made like
a palm-tree stump, unable to grow again, and not liable to arise in
the future. Therefore, prince, I have slept well.*

(Aṅguttara Nikāya 3:35)

And might not a householder be tormented by hatred or by delusion,
the Buddha goes on to ask, so that he would sleep badly? We, like
Hatthaka, can hardly deny the likelihood. Good sleep—or tranquility in
the larger sense—is not made certain by any material comfort or luxury
or sensual pleasure. The *Tathāgata*—the "one gone thus," the fully
enlightened Buddha—sleeps well because those baneful disturbances of

lust, hatred, and delusion, those fierce tormentors of the mind, have all been destroyed in him. He is clean and unburdened and empty of all defilements, and beside that tremendous fact the incidents of weather count for little. In his thin robes he is utterly at peace despite the frost and the wind.

The story in the Pāli Canon is brief; we are told little more; but the scene holds its shape in our imagination—grows more vivid, indeed, as the meaning makes its way deeper into us. We can picture the two figures in the frosty landscape. There is the cold wind hissing dismally in the trees; branches are creaking and rattling together; withered leaves are plucked loose and sent twirling through the empty, comfortless forest. But at ease on the rough, cold ground, on the thin spread of leaves, the Buddha tells the marveling Hatthaka that he sleeps well. And we know it is true.

How many wretched hours have we spent lying wakeful in the dark, desperately wanting and desiring and burning to no purpose? All our lives long we have been struggling to satisfy whatever passion that seizes us, rarely asking whence it comes or what good it serves. But now there rises before us this vision of peace not got by worldly pleasures, this tableau of spiritual beauty that lingers and inspires. By a few spare words, and by the tranquility of his own person in the desolate forest, the Buddha teaches sublime truth. That stillness, that purity within, is far above the rage of lust and far beyond all worldly luxury, but *there* lies freedom, in that direction.

Having searched and found suffering and its origin and its cessation and the way to its cessation, the Buddha tells us plainly, in terms that we can understand, what we ought and ought not to do in order to diminish our pain and increase our happiness. He does not expect us instantly to abandon all our pleasures and pursuits and become saints untouched by passion, but rather, by gradual practice in our daily lives, to discipline ourselves decently, to turn away from the unwholesome, to inquire into the workings of our minds, and to confirm for ourselves the radiant truths that he discovered.

The desperate, exhausted world dances on in a fever of passion and seemingly would have us, too, caught up in the same mad conflagration.

But shall we not step away to saner air, and listen to the Dhamma, and wander in the forest, as it were, with Prince Hatthaka on a cold, clear day? There, all burning done, all fever ended, the Tathāgata has slept well and over the senseless wind speaks his words of majesty and wisdom.

11. Undeclared Questions

IN ORDER PROPERLY TO understand Buddhism and to practice it for our welfare, we have to bear in mind the fundamental purpose for which the Buddha taught. We who first come upon Buddhism as adults during a spiritual or philosophical quest might assume, in our early enthusiasm, that we are going to discover here the answers to certain questions that seem to us very important. We are intellectually troubled, perhaps, and although we might like to practice religion heartily and confidently, we are reluctant to do so as long as we remain in doubt about various metaphysical, philosophical, or cosmological matters. We are curious; we are hungry for explanations; so we ask our questions when we get the chance, or else we drift about silently from book to book, hoping to find those questions somewhere neatly framed and succinctly answered and the way to a full spiritual life thereby opened to us.

Such an approach to Buddhism, as natural and reasonable as it seems, may result in some disappointment if we assume that the Buddha's purpose as the Enlightened One must have been to answer, consolingly, reassuringly, and fully, those questions that we in our private meditations have determined to be of moment. Where did we come from? What were we in the life before this one, if indeed we existed? How about in lives further back than that? Where will we go when this present life ends? Why is our personality the way it is? How big is the universe? When did it begin? Will it last forever? How many living beings exist? What exactly is life like in heaven or in hell? Will we be able to reach enlightenment? If so, how long will it take? These and many more questions—including very particular anxieties about our own moral standing or emotional make-up—concern us intensely, so we expect them to concern our spiritual teachers as well.

But if we study the Pāli Canon we soon come to learn that the Buddha, although he does indeed inform us of many things, does not necessarily satisfy all our curiosity. That is not his purpose. We may be eager for particular explanations, for imagined responses, but the Buddha's purpose is simply and strictly this: to put an end to suffering, to dukkha. All else is beside the point. He does not offer us the Dhamma just to inform us or educate us but to free us from suffering. Therefore the information, the knowledge, the education that he does impart are calculated for our progress toward that freedom. What is irrelevant to that progress the Buddha does not teach, even though we might desire it.

Examples of people who desire answers to irrelevant questions can be found in the Pāli Canon. In one notable case a certain bhikkhu named Mālunkyāputta gets worked up over a set of ten "speculative views" or abstruse questions that the Buddha has not explained to him, and he decides that if the Buddha will not explain them he will abandon his training as a monk and go back to lay life. The conflicting views that rankle him are these:

> *The world is eternal...the world is not eternal...the world is finite...the world is infinite...the soul is the same as the body...the soul is one thing and the body another...after death a Tathāgata exists...after death a Tathāgata does not exist... after death a Tathāgata both exists and does not exist...after death a Tathāgata neither exists nor does not exist.*
>
> (Majjhima Nikāya 63:2)

Mālunkyāputta approaches the Buddha, expresses his displeasure, and announces his ultimatum: either the Buddha will explain these questions and answer whether they are true or false or he, Mālunkyāputta, will leave the Sangha. He adds, moreover, the impudent remark that if the Buddha in fact does not *know* the answers to these questions, the straightforward thing is to admit that he does not know.

The Buddha, the Tathāgata, "the one gone thus," first of all gets Mālunkyāputta to acknowledge that he was never promised answers to these questions when he entered the Sangha. Then the Buddha, not at all to be pressured by anybody, says that if someone says he will give up the holy life unless he gets his answers, that person will surely die before he is ever satisfied. Matters that are "undeclared" by the Tāthāgata will remain so, and that is that.

The Buddha does, however, compassionately go on to give a simile designed to straighten out the deluded Mālunkyāputta. Suppose, he says, that a man were shot by a poisoned arrow, and his relatives should come to his aid and bring a surgeon to remove the arrow. But suppose the wounded man says he will not allow the arrow to be removed until he can find out who was the man who shot him, and what were his caste and his clan, and what he looked like, and where he lived, and what kind of bow he used, and what kind of arrow he used, and what kind of feathers were on the arrow, and what kind of point was on the arrow, and many other details besides. That man, the Buddha says, would die before he could get his questions answered. In the same way, someone who says he will abandon the holy life unless he is answered as he demands will die, too, never getting what he wants.

The Buddha then says that entertaining these speculative views makes the living of the holy life impossible, and he points out to the foolish monk the overwhelming fact of dukkha, to which he should be giving his attention:

> *Whether there is the view "the world is eternal" or the view "the world is not eternal," there is birth, there is aging, there is death, there are sorrow, lamentation, pain, dejection, and despair, the destruction of which I prescribe here and now.*
>
> (Majjhima Nikāya 63:6)

It is exactly the same with regard to the rest of these speculative views. Whether or not the world, the universe, or this plane of existence is finite or infinite, there are still birth and death and suffering. Whether or not the soul is identical with the body, the great perils of existence surround all people and their families. Whether or not a Tathāgata exists after death, suffering continues for living beings. And while humanity puzzles and argues over these and other rarefied, metaphysical matters, the Tathāgata is doing his practical work of explaining what needs to be explained and prescribing the way to destroy suffering. Knowing what is useful and what is not, he simply does not declare one way or the other with regard to such questions.

> *Why have I left that undeclared? Because it is unbeneficial, it does not belong to the fundamentals of the holy life, it does not lead to disenchantment, to dispassion, to cessation, to peace, to direct knowledge, to enlightenment, to Nibbāna. That is why I have left it undeclared.*
>
> (Majjhima Nikāya 63:8)

There are, we may well suppose, limitless oceans of possible knowledge; but relatively little of it could ever be useful in our own lives. The Buddha is concerned with what is most useful, what is most beneficial to us—the destruction of dukkha and the attainment of Nibbāna—and whatever has no bearing on that great project he does not discuss. He asks us instead to concentrate on what he does declare; namely, the truth of suffering, the truth of the origin of suffering, the truth of the cessation of suffering, and the truth of the way leading to the cessation of suffering. These things, he tells us, are beneficial and lead to Nibbāna. Like the man shot by the poisoned arrow, we are suffering from defilements within ourselves and should make haste to accept the help of the skillful surgeon, the Buddha.

On another occasion recorded in the Pāli Canon, the Buddha, asked by the ascetic wanderer Vacchagotta about this same set of ten questions, explains that such speculative views are not only irrelevant but also positively harmful:

> *Vaccha, the speculative view that the world is eternal is a thicket of views, a wilderness of views, a contortion of views, a vacillation of*

views, a fetter of views. It is beset by suffering, by vexation, by despair, and by fever....

(Majjhima Nikāya 72:14)

Then in identical terms the Buddha dismisses the view that the world is *not* eternal, likewise the views of the world as finite or as infinite. All of these speculations, in fact, he regards in the same way, as "a thicket of views"—an obstacle, a danger to be avoided.

The truth or untruth of any of these views is not the point. The welfare of living beings is the point. We might be very keen to know whether this world, this universe, this observable realm of being is eternal and whether it is of infinite extent. We might wonder whether what is called soul is the same or different from the physical body to which we suppose it to be attached. We might wonder whether an enlightened person, either the Buddha himself or one of his fully enlightened followers, will go on to exist in some imaginable form after death. These are intriguing questions; but realistically, amid the troubles and bereavements of our daily lives, amid our present errors and pains and hopes, do they matter at all? Being informed one way or the other, would we be any happier or more secure? Indeed, no possible answer to these questions could better our lives or prevent future suffering; therefore the Buddha declines to answer as we wish.

There are, we ought to recognize, matters that are altogether outside our experience, outside our comprehension (as unpleasant as it may be to admit that), and even outside of words and concepts entirely. Asked by Vacchagotta about the existence or nonexistence of a Tathāgata after death, the Buddha says that "reappears" or "does not reappear" or similar worldly terminology "does not apply." All that we know of in this universe, all that we can conceive of, is what is born, conditioned, and compounded. With regard to what is unborn, unconditioned, and uncompounded, words and concepts utterly fail. A Tathāgata who has finished his final life and passed away leaves no mark, no phenomenon, no means at all by which anyone could define him. Having finally abandoned the five aggregates—material form, feeling, perception, mental formations, and consciousness—he cannot be described in any worldly

way, so questions about his whereabouts after death are vain and meaningless. It is like asking whether a fire that has gone out has gone out to
the east, to the west, to the north, or to the south: no answer, no reck-
oning will serve in that case.

> *The Tathāgata is liberated from reckoning in terms of material*
> *form...feeling...perception...mental formations...consciousness....*
> *He is profound, immeasurable, hard to fathom like the ocean.*
>   (Majjhima Nikāya 72:20)

This is as far as the Buddha will go on the subject of what happens to
a fully enlightened person after death. Steady in his purpose, he never
accepts any of the offered alternatives. There is practical good to be done
in the human world, and he does it, teaching his followers how to
observe, how to contemplate, and how to act virtuously for the elimination of dukkha.

The search for spiritual peace is not simply a matter of striving to get
more indiscriminate knowledge about the universe. It is instead a matter of learning what questions are worth pursuing and deserve our attention. These are not always obvious within the clouds of our own desire,
bias, and curiosity, and we need the teaching of the Buddha to orient us
and urge us onward to discover fruitful truth on our own. The Buddha
tells us that we should ask pertinent and practical questions about what
is wholesome and unwholesome, what is blameless and blameable, what
should and should not be cultivated, and what kinds of actions lead to
what kinds of results. These are the sorts of meaningful questions that
the Buddha is always willing to listen to; and his rich and inspiring
answers fill up many pages of the Pāli Canon.

We are inquisitive beings—we wish to dispel at least some of the
tremendous mysteries that loom over our brief, troubled lives—and
that is not at all a bad wish, for certain kinds of knowledge will indeed
uplift us and relieve us of our sorrows. We just need to refine our purposes, pay respectful attention to wise counsel, and go on to practice the
Noble Eightfold Path with faith and energy. It may be that our fascination with abstruse questions is only the expression of deep unease

about our present, unguided, unsatisfactory situation. Loss of our beloved relatives, divorce, sickness of our children, business trouble, and conflict with our neighbors cause us incalculably more distress than not having answers to metaphysical questions. Not knowing what to do about our immediate troubles, we may rashly assume that relief from them exists behind this or that perceived mystery. Instead of pondering the imponderable, however, it would be wise to investigate and apply the accessible principles of harmlessness, benevolence, and mental purification that the Buddha so often emphasizes. These good principles, put into action, bring relief and understanding in natural course.

When we refrain from evil, for example, even in a very small way, such as cutting off the impulse to say something malicious, our healthy effort confers a balm on the mind. In the succeeding minutes we are free from the burning residue of malice and thus better able to meditate or just to observe the world clearly. When we do some small kindly act, the principle of cause and effect ensures that a measure of kindliness will come back upon us, making life a little more tranquil and manageable. When we reflect on the Four Noble Truths, we use our intelligence in the best way and gain inspiration to travel along the good path ascertained and lived by the Buddha and to observe the landmarks for ourselves.

We rely on the Buddha for advice on how to conduct ourselves wisely, so that by our own work and our own experience valuable truths will become clear to us. What the Buddha himself *knew* is beyond our range, unsayable and inconceivable, but from the record of his life we see that he had compassion and was able to point his disciples in the direction of deliverance from all suffering. This is what should matter to us.

Once, when dwelling in a certain grove, the Buddha picked up some leaves and asked his disciples which was greater, the number of leaves in his hand or the number of leaves in the grove overhead. The monks answered that the leaves in his hand were few with respect to the many in the the grove overhead. Then the Buddha said, "So too, bhikkhus, the things I have directly known but have not taught you are numerous, while the things I have taught you are few." The reason he did not teach those numerous things, he said, was that they were not beneficial and did not lead to enlightenment. What he did teach was the Four Noble Truths, which were indeed beneficial and did lead to enlightenment. He then concluded with an exhortation:

> *Therefore, bhikkhus, an exertion should be made to understand:*
> *"This is suffering"... "This is the origin of suffering"... "This is the*
> *cessation of suffering." An exertion should be made to understand:*
> *"This is the way leading to the cessation of suffering."*
>
> (Saṃyutta Nikāya 56:31)

In teaching the liberating Dhamma the Buddha reveals many valuable and useful things; he explains the processes at work in our lives; he shows, in the Four Noble Truths, the principles that produce our sorrow and our happiness, and he declares that an exertion should be made to understand them. It is wise to listen to what the Buddha says about the nature of suffering, but listening is not sufficient for our liberation. We must go on to make an effort, to exert ourselves, to strive intelligently along the path that he has explained. Always in the teaching of the Buddha we find this balance, this complementary discipline of listening to instruction and discovering truth for ourselves. We will not find our way out of the mazes of saṃsāra by trusting exclusively to our whims and tastes; and we will not find our way out just by studying doctrine; rather we must listen attentively to what the Buddha has to say and then use our own energy to move along the path that he has shown.

Liberation from suffering always depends on intelligent attention to the impersonal, natural process of cause and effect. As long as the defilements of greed, hatred, and delusion fester within us, there will be repeated birth and death and suffering of various kinds. If those defilements can be removed, there will be complete liberation at last. These axioms are easy enough to understand in the abstract, but we might still hesitate to practice the Dhamma because of doubts about our own personal prospects. "What about *me*?" we want to know. "If I devote myself to the Dhamma will I attain enlightenment?"

These questions, too, though they seem so pertinent to our welfare, can have no definite answer. Everything depends on conditions, and conditions change. It is as if, before setting out on a road to a distant country, we are requiring assurances and proofs that we will reach the destination we have envisioned, just *as* we have envisioned it, and in such time and with such conditions as we have previously approved. It is almost as if we ask to be shown the future before we will bestir ourselves in the present. We might admit the absurdity of such a desire and yet keep asking— longing for emancipation but postponing the necessary work.

We would be happy to know that our future enlightenment is certain, but the universe is simply not arranged that way. We are conditioned beings, in that we have come to this particular junction in time as a result of countless past actions, but our future state is not fixed because we are now and always free to perform new actions by body, speech, and mind. These new actions will have their own effects which may alter our existence little or much, for good or for bad. Enlightenment is *possible,* not certain. It depends on how well we manage to live according to the Noble Eightfold Path.

The Buddha was the masterful teacher who explained what we must do in order to set up conditions that will result in our happiness and eventually our liberation from the cycle of dukkha. The student, the follower of the Buddha, must make his own intelligent efforts for his own safety. There is no getting around this responsibility.

In the Pāli Canon there is the story of a certain brahmin who asks the Buddha whether all his disciples, after being taught by him, go on to attain Nibbāna. The Buddha replies that some do and some do not. This evidently touches on the common human wish to be sure of the future, because the brahmin then asks a question that might occur to anyone:

> *Master Gotama, since Nibbāna exists and the path leading to Nibbāna exists and Master Gotama is present as the guide, what is the cause and reason why, when Master Gotama's disciples are thus advised and instructed by him, some of them attain Nibbāna, the ultimate goal, and some do not attain it?*
>
> (Majjhima Nikāya 107:13)

To this the Buddha does not return an immediate answer. Instead, he asks the brahmin whether he is familiar with the road leading to the city of Rājagaha. When the brahmin says he is, the Buddha asks him to imagine what he would do if a traveler came to him and inquired as to how to get to Rājagaha. Suppose the brahmin shows the traveler the right road and then advises him of the landmarks he will see along the way: first a certain village, then a certain town, and then Rājagaha itself with its lovely features. But suppose that traveler, after being advised, should turn off to the left instead of going straight. And suppose another traveler should come, receive the same directions, go on by the right road and keep to it and then reach the city. Why then would it be that, although the city exists and the road exists and the brahmin has given directions, one traveler gets safely to the city and one does not?

The brahmin makes the obvious objection: "What can I do about that, Master Gotama? I am one who shows the way." The Buddha then points out the parallel:

> So too, brahmin, Nibbāna exists and the path leading to Nibbāna exists, and I am present as the guide. Yet when my disciples have been thus advised and instructed by me, some of them attain Nibbāna, the ultimate goal, and some do not attain it. What can I do about that, brahmin? The Tathāgata is one who shows the way.
> (Majjhima Nikāya 107:14)

The Tathāgata does not overrule the laws of nature; he does not revise the operation of the universe; he only teaches, and some heed his teaching and some do not. We who have heard of Nibbāna and aspire to reach it are daily and hourly making choices—whether to turn this way or that, whether to behave in one way or another, whether to act on some impulse or not to act—and these choices, far more than mere aspirations, determine our progress or lack of progress. We are free to get lost, in short, and we are also free to travel by the good path.

As we contemplate the horizons around us and begin to realize that safety from the sorrows of existence can and should be found, many sorts of questions will occur to us. We should attend to those that are practical and spiritually profitable. Is the world eternal? Is it not eternal? Is it finite? Is it infinite? The breezes of speculation blow back and forth without advantage, and meanwhile our actions of good or evil pile up and bring us joy or suffering. Since we are travelers, since we seek that lovely city free from pain, we ought to ask questions specific to that goal. What is wholesome? What is unwholesome? What deeds should we do and not do? The Tathāgata is one who shows the way. It is a good way, and it is right before us.

12. *A Cold Day with Much Sun*

Let us step boldly, shall we, into the awareness of a promising moment. Right now there is nothing but blue sky overhead—limitless, clean, and absolute. The old earth has dropped away below our upturned gaze, has vanished from our concern, as we take long, frosty breaths and admire unhurriedly that bright blue vastness. How many times before have we gotten lost in the contemplation of such a sky and imagined that in a moment we could look down again, cleansed of all our sorrows, and find ourselves in some fantastic new landscape of adventure? Vast, blue uncertainty prevails for a little while each time, until with a sigh we give up and resign ourselves to the earthly and the ordinary. But today for some reason the fresh, cold air and the radiance of the vacant heavens ring so magically upon our senses that we do not fall to dreaming, and when we do stop gazing upward we look down slowly and without disappointment, just letting the horizon rise gradually into view and welcoming it as if it does bring a wholly new season of inspiration. Let us determine to be alert. What now is this amazing earth we seem to see and hear and feel? What is this day alive around us?

Look, there are brown, wintry hills in the distance. Nearer at hand are slopes of drab forest still without leaves and a broad, muddy creek bordered by sycamores, and on this side of the creek a plain of short grass with park benches here and there and a few shrubs just starting to get green. It is March, a cold afternoon with no wind and much sun, and we are standing alone, enjoying these stark sensations even as we expect some current of worry to push us off balance once again. For this little while, at any rate, we seem to be getting along well enough on the simple perception of day and season and standing body; and we are not entirely sure whether we have not, after all, passed beyond old banality into a new and beautiful era.

It may be the chance harmony of natural elements today, or it may be just our whimsical will to behold the wonderful and the marvelous, but here we are, come to life with hope in this new hour, ready to go hiking off toward whatever seems good. There is a forsythia bush over there whose blossoming we could witness. There is the creek, whose ripples are redoubling the sun's blaze in splendid flashes. There is a squirrel, an emblem of vitality, bounding gracefully over the grass. Somewhere a few birds cry out in the huge void of the spring day, and now and then someone on a bicycle comes clicking along the crushed limestone path that crosses the field; but mostly there is just a semi-silence of great spaces and depths of time in which a few idlers like ourselves pace slowly or stand about with faces raised toward the sun.

It is, we suppose, the time for spring to be appearing with all its flourishes; but seasons never change with exact definition, and it seems for now we shall just have to deal with this stiff, cold day full of sunlight. The relative simplicity of the scene—indeed, the absence of many things—may actually heighten our gladness and anticipation. We have come to a new country, or at least our attitude is new. We are watching the world of sensation, not with any special hunger for amusement but with only a cool curiosity, an interest in significant things. What is this maze of shocking light before us? What is this chill of air on skin? What is this weight of a coat on our shoulders? We have names for these things; there is really no mystery about them; but still it is oddly pleasant to keep silent and turn a fresh regard here and there on the sparse furniture of the day.

This world of park and hill and sky does not yet overwhelm us with sensory profusion. If not entirely barren this afternoon, it is certainly austere. We scan the flat, cold field, look toward the forest with its brown solemnity streaked with the gray and white of sycamores, stare again at the empty sky, and return to the nearby creek and the forsythia bush. How much entertainment does the mind require? Not really very much, it seems, if we can keep a degree of balance. And in such moments as now, as we begin to plod meditatively over the soft, damp ground, we find ourselves wondering whether the objects we perceive ever contain anything in the way of entertainment themselves, or whether our fevers of desire and delight are only dreams, constructions of the mind. We may not be able to settle such questions this afternoon, but it is interesting to reflect that park benches, grass, creek, and forest come to us as patterns of sensations only, on which, without much consideration, we usually suppose a world of substance and durability. Today, with this strange, light mood upon us, it seems possible to get along gracefully without assuming so much—just taking sound and color and motion in mindful simplicity. If the scenery is a little stark, a little wintry still, that is no problem. It is not abundance, ultimately, that we require, but peace. Spring, coming slow or late, will work its changes without our worrying, so meanwhile should we not stay ready to contemplate, for the sake of our peace, whatever of beauty or meaning that may be appearing now?

By sights, sounds, smells, tastes, touches, and mental objects, the world becomes known to us; and yet how tenuous all of these are, how slight, how ephemeral. Today with the scenery so cold and fine and spare, it is not hard to believe it is empty of all substance—just conditions flashing wondrously on the screen of our consciousness. What is there to depend on here? We had best be attentive and see what we can learn from the wild dynamism of things.

The scene we look at now is vast and vacant, with the woods not quite blooming and the muddy creek shining and the blank sky displaying no clouds, no readable messages. It is all an exhilarating but baffling blend of sensations. Even these hands and feet of ours that are stirring about— we only know them by means of swift sensations that continually arise and pass away. All that we know of the world, indeed, comes from sensations; and if these sensations are, as they seem to be, transient, flickering, and empty, what shall we say of the world they represent? Thus our ruminations, wandering away over the landscape, lead us back to a deep old intuition, which the Buddha has explained and elaborated.

> *Then the Venerable Ānanda approached the Blessed One...and said to him: "Venerable sir, it is said, 'Empty is the world, empty is the world.' In what way, venerable sir, is it said, 'Empty is the world'?"*
>
> *"It is, Ānanda, because it is empty of self and of what belongs to self that it is said, 'Empty is the world.' And what is empty of self and of what belongs to self? The eye, Ānanda, is empty of self and of what belongs to self. Forms are empty of self and of what belongs to self. Eye-consciousness is empty.... Eye-contact is empty.... Whatever feeling arises with eye-contact as condition—whether pleasant or painful or neither-painful-nor-pleasant—that too is empty of self and of what belongs to self. The ear, Ānanda, is empty of self.... The nose.... The tongue.... The body.... The mind.... Whatever feeling arises with mind-contact as condition...that too is empty of self and of what belongs to self."*
>
> (Saṃyutta Nikāya 35:85)

Sometimes, as now, when we contemplate the airiness and changeability of the objects that appear to us, we return to the idea—or the apprehension—that all this world might ultimately be unreal, phantasmal, empty, or imaginary. Here the Buddha is indeed saying that the world is empty, but empty in a specific way that we might not have considered. It is not empty in the sense of being nonexistent or without reality or meaning; it is not just imaginary; rather it is "empty of self and of what belongs to self." This world that we have habitually taken as a dwelling place of self or ego, as a backdrop for the performances of static beings, exists as a flood of changing conditions with no center, no cohering, lasting identity to cling to and own. Our individual existence in this flood is not static, either. The elements of nature flow on, and we flow on, too, as patterns of ceaselessly changing conditions; and within the patterns, within the fluctuating sensations of any moment, no self or ego, no fixed, unchanging essence, can be found.

It is strange enough to be told that the world is empty of self and of what belongs to self, but the Buddha here outlines further amazing depths. What exactly is this world? It is the eye and visible forms, the ear and sounds, the nose and smells, the tongue and tastes, the body and tactile impressions, the mind and mental objects. It is the process of perception as well as perceptions themselves.

The eye, the Buddha says, is empty of self and of what belongs to self. It is not hard to understand that the eye, being but a temporary construction, has no inherent essence and owns nothing; it is simply an organ that functions in a certain way. Visible forms—temporary patterns of light—are also empty of self. Eye-consciousness, the type of consciousness that arises when visible forms strike the intact organ, is also empty of self. Eye-contact is the name for the meeting, the conjunction, of eye and visible forms and consciousness; and it too, being simply a process, not a static thing, can harbor no self. Out of contact a certain kind of feeling arises, which may be pleasant or unpleasant or neutral; but feeling, looked at analytically, is just another conditioned, dependent, transitory phenomenon and thus is likewise devoid of abiding identity. Wherever we turn in visual experience we find dynamic conditions rising and falling but no self or ego within or behind the conditions.

The Buddha goes on to describe in the same terms the other sense bases and the processes of perception that follow from them. The ear, being impermanent and liable to disintegration, holds no discrete essence, no ego or self; likewise the sounds that enter the ear; likewise the whole process of auditory perception. Nose, tongue, body, and mind, too, should be seen just as what they are, without supposing an owner or inhabitant of the flood of events. The nose deals with smells, the tongue with tastes, the body with tactile impressions, and the mind with mental objects. In all cases there is a flux of impersonal conditions running on, which we can summarize as "the world."

When we crave and grasp at the apparent pleasures of this world we suffer, for they are all transitory, without substance, and incapable of giving us durable satisfaction. When we suppose that identity or self or permanent security must reside in this or that complex of temporary sensation, we continue to blunder around in frustration, because the world is actually empty of that for which we yearn. But since the world is empty in this sense, not harboring any literal, possessable ego, when we turn away from our fascination with ego we may begin to understand the beautiful freedom toward which the Buddha points. If sights, sounds, smells, and all other sensations and feelings are indeed devoid of "me" or anything belonging to "me," then when they change, as they surely will, we need not suffer if we do not cling.

Out on foot in this fine, cold spring day, we notice emptiness first of all in the stark, unpopulous landscape, in the barren, lonely woods and the featureless park lawns and the signless sky. But as we drift along in the sunlight, forgetting or simply disregarding our tiresome worries, we also discover a kind of emptiness, a kind of freedom, just in the act of disinterestedly noticing grass, water, woods, and sky. These things do not belong to us, so for a little while at least we do not trouble ourselves about them; we observe and find them beautiful, perhaps, in a tranquil, meditative sense, but we discover, as we move and look and listen and breathe, that there is no need to own them or wish them more lovely or graceful. Such an attitude well suits the lawful course of nature. All things will change, and it is healthy to be mindful of the fact, for it keeps us from flinging ourselves, for comfort or delight or security, on that which is helpless to support us.

We cannot reasonably fasten on any transient aspect of the empty world, any wisp of sensation, as an eternal, comforting ego or self; but this fact of emptiness, rightly regarded, may inspire us to search for what is better and nobler:

> *Bhikkhus, there are these two kinds of search: the noble search and the ignoble search. And what is the ignoble search? Here someone being himself subject to birth seeks what is also subject to birth; being himself subject to aging, he seeks what is also subject to aging; being himself subject to sickness, he seeks what is also subject to sickness; being himself subject to death, he seeks what is also subject to death; being himself subject to sorrow, he seeks what is also subject to sorrow; being himself subject to defilement, he seeks what is also subject to defilement.*

> (Majjhima Nikāya 26:5)

What is it that is subject to birth, aging, sickness, death, sorrow, and defilement? The Buddha says it is "objects of attachment"—the members of our families, our possessions, the various forms of our worldly wealth. All these, though they may indeed bring us some temporary happiness, are still lamentably insecure and subject to dissolution. We engage in an "ignoble search" when, being of a fragile, temporary, impermanent nature ourselves, we seek our safety in that which has exactly the same nature. This kind of search is endless and full of trouble. Fortunately, there is another kind of search:

> *And what is the noble search? Here someone being himself subject to birth, having understood the danger in what is subject to birth, seeks the unborn supreme security from bondage, Nibbāna; being himself subject to aging...sickness...death...sorrow...defilement...he seeks the unborn supreme security from bondage, Nibbāna. This is the noble search.*
>
> (Majjhima Nikāya 26:12)

What kind of search are we engaged in on this brilliant, breezeless afternoon in March? And to what kind of search have we devoted our past years? Maybe we would rather not supply answers to these questions right now, preferring to stroll on peacefully through the indifferent sunshine. But here alone by the creek under the sycamores we find that no great fears attack us, and we might well muse a little on this idea of a search. Admittedly, there have been countless hours and days in which we have burned with purposes of an entirely mundane and trivial sort, never lifting our heads from the level of attachment and amusement. Still, there have been finer moments, such as these, when we gaze at the sky and take in some brave breaths and reflect on possibilities beyond the chattering of the senses. We have come out here for exercise, seeking recreation of a sort, wishing to refresh ourselves with the slight pleasure of wandering under a dazzling blue sky; and if these are not the highest purposes, at least they have led us into the vicinity of meditation and given us the chance to apply our minds to serious themes. We have learned from the Buddha that a noble search is possible, and when it happens that we glimpse the hollowness of the objects around us, we feel a rare lightness, a readiness to be off and searching for that which lies beyond birth and aging and all sad states of being.

Maybe, indeed, we are already searching. This afternoon we walk from one unimportant spot to another on the green plain by the creek, not because any item of scenery especially intrigues us but because we wish to try out different vantage points for our contemplation. Up in the woods the barely budding trees assure us of a rich blooming ahead—and assure us also of another fading. There is, alas, no security in the woods. Down the gravel path in another direction the sunlit park lands fall away into a boundless distance that makes us think of freedom in more than a spatial sense. This body, being healthy, might hike a long way down that path; but by what thorns and fences is the mind still balked? What sorrows and fears are still unremedied within us? We are looking across the landscape of perception, dimly and uncertainly, for a way out of all affliction.

When we have the Dhamma in mind the sounds and forms and motions of nature come upon our senses with new significance. Once we might have hoped merely to enjoy our perceptions more keenly, but now perhaps we begin to read them as emblems of the character of the universe. Nothing of the world of sensation can sustain us very long. Nothing of what is born, compounded, conditioned, and put together will last. Therefore, for real security, we will have to seek what is beyond all that—"the unborn supreme security from bondage."

The emptiness of the world as described by the Buddha is not some gloomy vacuity or negation but an encouraging sign of our fundamental freedom. Because all phenomena are transitory, variable, and mutually conditioned—not frozen forever in any state—and because as conscious beings we can always exercise volition, we are capable of bringing about wholesome change in our lives. And if, through daily practice of the good principles of the Noble Eightfold Path, we can reduce some of the defilements and dissatisfactions that trouble us, why should we not look further and seek the highest good, Nibbāna?

The Noble Eightfold Path is not just a set of tasks before us but rather the best, the most ennobling, way for us to walk through our present condition of life toward a brightening future, even toward complete emancipation. We have, surely, obstacles before us; but on a day when all the world stands in the March sunlight so empty, fugitive, and ephemeral—and yet so beautiful—we might consider that those obstacles have the same tenuous, changeable nature. What attaches us to them but our own clinging? The Buddha says that he teaches the Dhamma "for the sake of final Nibbāna without clinging" (*Saṃyutta Nikāya* 35:75). It is through nonclinging that the mind is liberated; and since the ordinary, worldly person by nature and habit grasps and clings to the perceived world, the Buddha trains his disciples to observe mindfully the true conditions of the world so that they will become disenchanted with and let go of what is impermanent, unsatisfactory, and empty of self.

Can we observe mindfully? Now there is the sound of our shoes scraping through sticks alongside the creek. There is the cold of the air when we move and the warmth of the March sun when we pause to gaze at the muddy water. We notice, when we pay attention, breath and heartbeat and the other strains and stretches of a mortal body. Out of the wild flood of perceptions we put together our picture of body and mind, of park, woodland, and creek, with great gray and white sycamores rising into a sky empty of everything but blue.

Let us just straggle along the flowerless bank of the creek, not regretting the absence of flowers, taking no care to seek out charming scenery only, but just watching as well as we can with detachment the procession of empty elements through our senses. The eye and forms, the ear and sounds, the nose and smells, the tongue and tastes, the body and tangible impressions, the mind and mental objects, the various kinds of consciousness, the pleasant and unpleasant and neutral feelings—to these we have clung too long, hoping to find self among them. These are "the world"—a troublesome burden. Why should we try to carry it? How much better to walk freely and unacquisitively, uplifted by the thought of liberation.

If this forsythia bush here is blossoming when we pass we will admire it, to be sure. If it is not, we need not worry, we need not delay our walk by hankering for what is not. Spring will overtake us soon enough— and pass us by as well. We as changing beings can put no rightful claim on the changing forsythia bush or on any lovely element of impermanent nature; our only power is power over our kamma, our action by body, speech, and mind; and that is what, despite the turmoil of the universe, can bring us peace.

Now we are plodding along the creek bank, noting green shoots amid the mud and sticks. The creek gets shallow in one place, and there the murky water pours briskly over rocks in the sunlight. In another place a sagging branch of a tree trails in the current, collecting an unlovely clot of leaves that bobs slowly, almost with a kind of grace, as if following some subtle pulse of time. From the opposite, undercut bank, masses of fine roots hang in the air, and here and there greater roots jut out. The trees above stand on these failing supports, leaning out above the ever-moving water, giving us more reasons to ponder impermanence.

The March sky is still unsullied by any cloud or bird or airplane, still a blank, blue field of uncertainty, a void in which, gazing too raptly, we get disoriented. Down here on the human level, for all the crumbling of impermanent things, we can make our way more certainly, guided by the good Dhamma. Creek and sky and cold March earth are not ours—we need make no effort to take hold of them; they will flow on in any case. And flowing on, not seized by us, how could they make us suffer? The sights, sounds, smells, and other sensations by which we contrive to know the world are merely phenomena dependently arisen and sure to change. They will not obey us, and meanwhile more rewarding work awaits us.

Though we are subject to birth, subject to aging, sickness, death, sorrow, and defilement, we do not have to remain so. Should we rouse ourselves from winter only to repeat last summer's folly? We can, if we wish, set out on the noble search for the supreme security from bondage. Look now, the heavens are still blue and brilliant, and the sun lights up the changing earth well enough for our purposes. It is, we cannot doubt, an excellent day for adventure.

13. Dust and Excuses

W HEN THE BUDDHA, newly enlightened, sat beneath a tree and considered whether he should teach the sublime Dhamma he had discovered, he looked out over the world compassionately, with the eye of a Buddha, comprehending the various natures of beings.

> *The Blessed One saw beings with little dust in their eyes and with much dust in their eyes, with keen faculties and with dull faculties, with good qualities and with bad qualities, easy to teach and diffi-cult to teach, and a few who dwelt seeing blame and danger in the other world.*
>
> (Saṃyutta Nikāya 6:1)

Although the work promised to be arduous, although ignorance lay heavy upon the multitudes of creatures moving in the cycle of birth and death, the Buddha decided, out of compassion, to teach. There were, he saw, some who were capable of understanding the Dhamma if they heard it. He then spent the remaining forty-five years of his life travel-ing on foot over the valley of the Ganges, teaching the Dhamma to peo-ple of all social classes and administering and instructing the Sangha, the monastic order of monks and nuns, so that the path to liberation would still be made known after this, his final life, was done.

From those early days till now, enlightenment has never been a cer-tainty for anybody; it depends on the fulfillment of the Noble Eightfold

Path, which is always a matter for individual striving. We who now begin to learn the Dhamma and consider undertaking the noble search for liberation might wonder, as we remember our weaknesses, whether or not we are among those with much dust in their eyes. We might wonder whether our faculties are sharp enough for efficacious meditation or whether our will power can ever conquer our laziness. Would it be pointless for us, weak as we are, fickle as we are, to take up this religion with serious resolve?

A good way to approach these questions would be to reflect, before all else, that the Buddha, the Enlightened One, the Tathāgata, knew what he was doing. He was not going to exert himself pointlessly. There would have been for him no reason to announce a doctrine that was too difficult for anybody to comprehend, so the fact that he did teach and continued to teach for the rest of his life signifies his confidence both in the Dhamma and in the capabilities of human beings. He meant to do good and he accomplished it. Perfectly comprehending the fears and lusts of humanity, the Buddha taught the Dhamma because he knew it was the cure for all those fears and lusts. There were indeed those in the world who could quickly understand and realize the Dhamma; but there was also the fact of impermanence: things will change; minds will change; what is feeble now may grow strong; he who scoffs or despairs may at length gain faith.

We see from the history of the Buddha's life related in the Pāli Canon that many who initially doubted or opposed the Buddha were brought around to glad acceptance when they had heard and thought over the wisdom he imparted. Now as then, people have differing amounts of dust in their eyes, and none of us can be sure that our future will turn out just as we wish; but as we all possess the power of volition, it is possible for us to become wiser and nobler. If we listen to wisdom, the listening will help us. If we practice what we have heard, the practice will help us. Spiritual vision clears up and vigor spreads through our limbs when we repeatedly make virtuous efforts. Obviously, not everybody, right now, is going to practice, appreciate, or take interest in the Dhamma, however skillfully taught, because the tastes and faculties of individuals are various and unpredictable; but if we have disciplined ourselves so far as to inquire seriously into the Dhamma, we may reasonably think that, having accomplished this much, we can accomplish more.

On one occasion related in the Pāli Canon, a certain headman of a village asks why, if the Buddha has compassion for living beings, "he teaches the Dhamma thoroughly to some, yet not so thoroughly to others." The Buddha explains by means of a simile, saying that a farmer might have three fields—one excellent, one of middling quality, and one inferior, "rough, salty, with bad ground." In which field, the Buddha asks, would the farmer first sow his seed? The headman replies that he would first sow seed in the excellent field, next in the field of middling quality, and then, if there were some seed left over, possibly in the field of inferior quality, since it might at least produce some fodder for cattle.

The Buddha then goes on to liken the three types of field to three types of people:

> *Headman, just like the field that is excellent are the bhikkhus and bhikkhunīs to me. I teach them the Dhamma that is good in the beginning, good in the middle, and good in the end, with the right meaning and phrasing; I reveal the holy life that is perfectly complete and pure. For what reason? Because they dwell with me as their island, with me as their shelter, with me as their protector, with me as their refuge.*
>
> (Saṃyutta Nikāya 42:7)

The Buddha then says that his male and female lay followers are like the field of middling quality, and he teaches them the Dhamma, too, because they too dwell with him as their island, their shelter, their protector, their refuge. The ascetics, brahmins, and wanderers of other sects he likens to the field of poor quality, but to them also he teaches the same good Dhamma. Why does he do that? "Because," he says, "if they understand even a single sentence, that will lead to their welfare and happiness for a long time."

The monks and nuns who live under the direct guidance of the Buddha receive from him the most thorough instruction, because they have already dedicated themselves to realization of the Dhamma; they have renounced the world to pursue the noble search. But the Buddha, being compassionate toward all beings, teaches the same Dhamma also to the ordinary lay men and women who follow him in faith. And even where effort might appear hopeless, even among those who are indifferent or unsympathetic, the Buddha teaches the Dhamma, because it is possible that such persons might comprehend something—even a single sentence—and even that would be a blessing for them. They might in time come back to listen with sincerity.

Two things are especially noticeable in this episode. First, in all cases the Buddha acts out of disinterested compassion for the welfare and happiness of beings, even though not all beings understand or return his kindness. That is just how a Tathāgata behaves; that is his noble nature. Second, though perfectly mindful of the infirmities of beings, the Buddha teaches the Dhamma as something worthwhile and beneficial even if it is not appreciated at first. Correct knowledge of the Dhamma is a potential that one might later recognize and develop, with fortunate results.

We might possibly have a lot of dust in our spiritual eyes; we might have bad qualities; we might be hard to instruct—but all these are conditioned and transient characteristics that need not remain, that need not continue. From the very beginning of his career, the Buddha, aware of the flaws of living beings, aware of their varying capabilities, kindly taught the Dhamma to all who were willing to listen and made sure, through the institution of the Sangha, that the Dhamma would remain available in the future for seekers of the good. When we today discover the Dhamma, even in imperfect outline, we become, like so many others, beneficiaries of the Buddha's work of compassion. We discover the possibility of our own reform and spiritual development, and also the possibility of our stagnation or decline if we fail to act rightly. What sort of choices shall we make? For indeed, no one can avoid making choices. Every hour is full of choices, decisions, intentions, volitions of one kind or another. The right kind, explained to us by the Buddha, will serve to cleanse us of dust.

But suppose our personal failings or our entrenched opinions are such that we think we cannot exert ourselves to the extent that the Buddha asks—what shall we do? Shall we resign ourselves to our present lamentable condition—to the poor condition of our soil—and simply wait for a fortuitous change in our nature to come about in time? This is an appealing idea but a bad one. For one thing, skill and conviction do not assemble themselves by chance. They must be cultivated. For another thing, there is a shadowy borderland between modesty and timidity. If we insist on our inability to practice the Dhamma right now, is it really because we are so exceptionally modest or is it because pleading weakness makes a pleasant excuse for fear or laziness? We might find it convenient to say, to others or only to ourselves, "Oh, I wish I could be more serious about Buddhism. I wish I could keep the precepts and meditate. But, oh well, I just don't seem to have what's necessary!" By this we mean to imply that nobody could possibly blame us or expect anything of us, since we are admitting our frailty with commendable candor. More likely, though, we are just anxious to escape a moral challenge because that challenge looks difficult.

Certainly we all have failings, and certainly misgivings about our capabilities are better than arrogant presumptions of spiritual superiority, but we should not belittle ourselves to the point of giving up all religious striving. We should not represent ourselves as weaker than we are or take inertness as a virtue. If we have indeed felt something of the brilliance and beauty of the Dhamma, we are already launched into another stage of development, wherein we should begin to see our rightful tasks.

We have all long known, in our best moments, that we ought to make ourselves into worthier human beings, that whatever virtues we possess should not be allowed to waste away but should be consciously increased, and that our inmost imperfections should not be allowed to fester and spoil our character but should be erased. Why is it then, we might wonder in these same best moments, that we have done so little to accomplish this? While we will, more than likely, privately acknowledge various weaknesses, we will probably not admit to *total* helplessness and incompetence. That would be too abject—and false, besides. We do have a certain measure of determination and strength, and we do have certain honorable intentions, which hitherto, it may be, have found no satisfactory direction. Now, when we have had the good fortune of hearing something of the Buddha's teaching, it is like healthy seeds falling on long-barren soil. Now something good is growing, be it lush or be it sparse, which can thrive if given good care. Our honorable intentions, of which we become more conscious, can find their direction here in the ancient and ever-fresh Dhamma.

But even when we have honorable intentions, and even when we know we are really not too weak spiritually to practice the Dhamma, we might still find obstacles—and with them, excuses—in the ordinary, clamorous business of life. What with the needs of our children, the wearying demands of work and school, the endless household duties, the social engagements, the family recreations, and our pastimes and hobbies, there is simply no *time,* we think, for much in the way of religious practice. Since formal meditation or study of the Pāli Canon or attendance at Buddhist temples or even deep reflection on our spiritual situation will require, as we think, great islands of free, uninfringed leisure, how could we manage to do more than we do already?

Behind this question there lies, perhaps, something of a misunderstanding of the nature of the Dhamma. To practice the Noble Eightfold Path is not to add another item to our daily agenda. To pursue the noble search for the cessation of suffering is not to neglect the fair conduct of our daily lives—it is to ease and beautify that fair conduct. As it is, we are struggling through household duties with the idea of eventually reaching some secure peace and satisfaction, but the means we employ seem strangely to put off peace and satisfaction indefinitely. The Noble Eightfold Path, if taken up seriously, helps us to fulfill our worldly duties with more grace and less agitation, and guides us at the same time toward higher purposes.

The principle of right action, for example, keeps us behaving in a harmless way that will cause no offense to others and no trouble and remorse for ourselves. Right speech serves us in daily life by smoothing all social relations and refining our own character. Right livelihood ensures that we will be honest, inoffensive, and scrupulous in all business affairs, which contributes to a good reputation. All the factors of the path deserve our diligent attention because they help us in mundane matters even as they lead us toward the final release from all suffering.

If we find our time too limited for all we would like to do (and nearly everybody does), by what standard do we choose what to attend to and what to forgo? There are, to be sure, many hours that must be dedicated to practical necessities like work, household chores, and care of our children, but what about the rest? We all apportion our time and our attention, as far as we can, according to our pleasure; so if, for example, we habitually choose to seek entertainment instead of studying or meditating or visiting a Buddhist temple, we can hardly complain that circumstances compel us to neglect the Dhamma. We choose, that is all. We act according to our will, and results naturally follow. As it happens, even the practical necessities are not so beyond the realm of our choice as we may think, because, while we do have to perform certain duties during certain hours, these can be done with or without mindfulness and concentration, with or without kindness, with or without self-effacement, honor, and compassion.

Another excuse for not practicing that we might have ready at hand, in case the others weaken, is that we are still not *sure* about the Dhamma, and thus, while we admire the principles of the Noble Eightfold Path, we are not quite ready to employ them very seriously. Who could blame us for our sensible caution? This is another attitude that sounds reasonable until we realize that the Noble Eightfold Path is not so much a set of doctrines to be believed as a program for sound and healthy action. The follower of the Dhamma is encouraged to investigate and test and confirm for himself its truth. If we do not investigate, how could we ever come to know?

Making excuses, vacillating, temporizing, and seeking relief from doubt in distractions do not protect us from error; they throw up more dust into our eyes. We will be making choices—and maybe errors—in any event, every day we live. Shall we choose according to thoughtless passions or firm ideals? Having heard something of the Dhamma, and having felt the undeniable touch of wisdom, we should realize that our faculties, frail though they may be, are good enough for perceiving what is necessary.

If we consider our mortal situation as a whole, from a certain philosophical distance, we ought to be able to see that, because we are still subject to birth, aging, sickness, death, sorrow, and defilement, we have no good excuse for complacency. As it stands now, suffering for us is imminent, and suffering will certainly come again unless its cause is removed; thus the Dhamma is a necessity for our future welfare, not just an incidental advantage. Despite the gaudy distractions that tempt us, we feel from time to time the intuition that the actions we are doing—in carelessness or in considered spite or kindness—will have someday, if not soon, a definite effect. What kind of life, what kind of goodness or misery, will close around us?

Long ago, when the Buddha first attained enlightenment, he saw among the different kinds of beings "a few who dwelt seeing blame and danger in the other world." These, he knew, would be apt students who could benefit from the Dhamma. Have we ever felt that stimulating apprehension about the possible results of unwholesome kamma? If so, if we suspect that our actions will bring corresponding results to us in this world and will determine our next destination after death, we must surely realize that to be safe and happy in the future we must find a way of wisely governing our actions now. This way is the living of the Noble Eightfold Path. This is good work that should not be postponed.

We need to feel the operation of the Dhamma in our lives for the sake of our own tranquility right now as well as for the sake of our future advancement in wisdom. Moreover, we have many lively cares for the effects we produce on others in daily life. How our relatives, our friends, and our children regard us is a matter that powerfully concerns us. We wish to leave some legacy more important than money or property—some appreciable legacy of love, wisdom, and trustworthy guidance—because by so doing we believe we can confer meaning and value on what might otherwise be just a hectic and useless spate of years. This aim cannot be accomplished by any manipulation of the material world, no matter how clever or zealous. It requires the betterment of our character.

We worry about our children, wondering whether we have equipped them well enough for life. Have we fostered in them a sense of honor and reverence? Have we taught them to know what is noble and what is base? Have we pointed out to them an unfailing standard of rightness to believe in? How could we, though? How could we teach what we have never learned? Before any true satisfaction, for the good of others and our own good, there must come the work, the striving, the dedicated pursuit of virtue, concentration, and wisdom in our own experience. Whenever we look beyond worldly power, wealth, and pleasure for meaningful goals, we find ourselves brought around again to the timeless Dhamma and to our own responsibility for practicing it. We who wish to leave something valuable to our children must understand that we can leave nothing we have not already gained. Wisdom is a quality won by private reflection, by learning from others, and by the cultivation of the mind by means of the Dhamma.

We who live surrounded by death require for our peace that Dhamma which leads on past death to the Deathless, to Nibbāna; and fortunately that Dhamma remains available in the world, thanks to the Buddha, who first taught it, and to the Sangha, which has preserved it for all these centuries. We doubt our own strength, it may be; we blink at the dust in our eyes and sigh gloomily; we make excuses and hope our conscience will settle down; but again and again, from the first moment we comprehend something of the majestic Dhamma, there comes this brave impulse to know more, to cross the limits of fear, to take a hand in the making of our destiny.

Long ago the Buddha, out of compassion for the suffering of living beings, made his decision to teach and then walked, alone, under the indifferent sun, to the city of Benares. In a park there five ascetic wanderers one day saw him coming toward them—a man they had known before, now somehow changed. What had been a private illumination was about to be given to the world; an epoch of freedom was about to begin. The Buddha sat down with them and spoke these words: "Listen, bhikkhus, the Deathless has been attained. I shall instruct you, I shall teach you the Dhamma." They did listen, and he did teach, and from that hour the beleaguered, shadowed world began to brighten.

Words are just flickerings of intelligence through space, but the words the Buddha spoke that day did not die out without remainder. Heard and understood and cherished, they were taken up and passed on, mind to astonished mind, over that country and beyond, through that day and year and beyond, like seeds rising up in a wind. What was the chance that we, so far away over the obliterating centuries, would ever hear the wisdom that he spoke? But we have heard it. Some words, at least, have settled into our minds; some seeds have fallen on our fields. May this soil prove fertile. May we make it so.

14. Investigations in the Evening

IKING TOWARD HOME well after sunset, coming up a weedy path from woods and fields, we begin to notice the tranquility of nature around us, the way the elements seem to compose themselves for the evening—calming down gradually, coming closer to stillness, reaching almost a kind of silent strength and poise as the light fades. After a touch of storminess, the breeze has fallen away, and the heavy leaves of summer have stopped swaying. The birds, after a little more flutter and noise, begin to disappear.

We sense again, after the distractions of the day, the swing of natural conditions, the motion of profound and timeless processes around our tiny lives. As the gray darkens in the east, stars appear, and the immensity of the universe becomes once again visible, while the scent of vegetation grows stronger and sweeter, enveloping us in a primeval atmosphere. The earth beneath our tired steps is massive and ancient—something to be counted on not for safety but perhaps for evidence of great natural certainties beyond our human trembling. We have, we realize, a kind of faith in the turning of the earth and in the flight of stars. We are strangely abashed and quieted this evening in the experience of such faith, but we are not comforted; we feel awe, not understanding, as we listen, stare, and smell the influences around us. How might we read deeper through these looming realities? How might we acquire a faith that actually comforts and inspires us who are mortal and temporary?

The truths taught by the Buddha often seem to us much like the natural laws we sometimes glimpse—they move like a subtle wind through our minds, swaying our sensibilities, until we realize at least what it is we need and have not yet secured. Knowledge of doctrine we may have in some degree, but faith in that knowledge is still faint; and thus, to do us any good, it must somehow be brought to maturity.

Mere growth there is, all around us, and corresponding decay. The long grasses whipping at our knees throw out new stems and leaves all the way to autumn and rise again vigorous in the spring. Endless growth goes on in this immense cycling of nature, but we, meanwhile, have not grown into certainty; we feel no faith automatically flowering from the passage of years. If, then, we are ever to acquire a full-grown, comforting faith in the Dhamma, how shall we find it? And how will it develop, if it ever does? Will it turn out to be as firm as the limestone cliffs in the hillsides here or as subtle and intuitive as these colors that pass through the air at dusk? Will we ever know faith in the way we know our own heartbeat or breathing, referring easily at any moment to a certainty within us?

Surely mature faith must be more than just an intellectual assent, more than just the harboring of some quantity of information about reality. Theoretical approval of a doctrine we can retract at any time—it has not cost us much and is easily redirected—but the greater faith we instinctively reach for must be a matter of breath and strength boldly expended, of actions consciously done and results bravely faced. We want to feel that we move in a landscape whose outlines at least we understand, whose dangers are superable, whose dimensions and meanings have been well measured by others before us. We desire the conviction that, although we have not yet discovered all that might be discovered, the standards by which we act are good and true.

Faith that sometimes springs up in us concerning very small matters, like the return of crocuses in early spring, or inarticulate faith in the majesty of the universe, or even religious faith just imagined, never actually possessed, still suggests the possibility of fullness; and although we will debate anxiously what the exact constituents of mature faith should be, we know, in our most honest reflections, that we must achieve it in good measure for a peaceful life. For too long, perhaps, we have lived in an arid postponement of faith, always guessing, evading, improvising, sorting through exhausting choices, still ignorant of the shadowy regions from which arise our impulses to go this way or that. Certainly any intelligent, reflective person wishes to find rich truth, to discover finally in experience the real character of the universe; but if we have not yet succeeded in this, we ought not to think that all comfort is lost to us or that there can be no peace or trust in noble standards. Faith is still attainable. Buddhist faith, even incipient and tentative, is a strong and guiding quality that can support us across dark spaces until our steps are sure.

In our uncertainty about what, if any, standards are really trustworthy, we might feel frustrated and uneasy, because it seems that to believe or even to test any standards we must commit ourselves to following them—and following is exactly what we are determined *not* to do until we can believe. We wanly hope that belief will someday arise spontaneously from experience, but surely the confirming experience can only come when we believe enough to act. Thus we dither and postpone, while fear and longing chase each other around and around. Will this dilemma always torment us? Can there ever be a sound, logical beginning to faith?

In the teaching of the Buddha we find explanations of the working of the universe, stories of wonder and courage, and beautiful, reasoned advice on how to behave for the increase of happiness. Listening to these or reading these, even with a doubting, uncommitted mind, lays in our hands innumerable threads of thought that can lead us to deeper investigation. A logical beginning to faith can happen when we pay attention to the right things in the right way. For some this beginning might be simple intellectual enthusiasm for some appealing aspect of the Dhamma, for others something as quiet as intuition or emotional attraction to the ideals of Buddhist tradition. Such favorable feelings are not sufficient in themselves to build up reliable religious faith, and not to be taken as guarantees of truth; but they might cause our attention to stick for more than a moment on some worthy theme, some inspiring story, or some insightful admonition. Then, when we contemplate the teaching seriously and follow clear lines of Dhamma out into the breathing, living world, we meet with convincing experience.

A beautiful idea that reaches us from without, a gift of words, might appeal to our personal tastes and might set off surprising reflections that make us turn to find evidence in the pedestrian scenes of daily life. This, when it happens, is a good thing, for nothing convinces us more than hours alertly lived through and mindfully observed. Thinking or reasoning, although very necessary, can give us no final assurance by itself and must be matched to the immediate farrago of perceptions. An idea held and contemplated will change, perhaps, will disappear or come to sudden vividness when tested by sights and sounds and smells and all the rest of the daily sensory panorama.

This doctrine of impermanence, for example—is it only a distant, irrelevant theory or does it apply right now to our immediate, individual, experienced world? Does it show itself this very evening as we climb up out of the woods toward the fringes of our neighborhood? Let us pause to look. Here the breeze that blew all day as if it could never stop has mysteriously failed and given way, for now, to stillness in the soft summer atmosphere. There is a flux of faint colors in the trees and grass and sky as the light weakens, and an irregular bunching and streaming of cars on a distant highway, and an unseen bird's call that breaks into the stillness as if to announce some new inspiration in nature but only warbles for a moment in the old, affecting, inconclusive way, and ceases.

Looking to the west now, we can barely glimpse a few insects flying above the grass, rising and dipping, darting and circling restlessly against the last red radiance in the sky. A smell of woods, mowed lawns, and summer flowers comes and goes, assuming now an earthy, antique intensity around us. As our path rises and falls through the country, gnats and mosquitoes and delicate lines of spider web lightly touch us and notify us of change, of variety, of the underlying unrest and complication of the universe. However much the earth this evening assumes an attitude of peace—or however much, in our weariness, we wish to see it so—we are reminded by the roaming insects and the turning sky that nowhere have we yet found any fixed, unchanging reality, any firm background to our being. As we approach the houses of our neighborhood we see more beams from automobiles swaying and swooping, broken by the trees and houses. We hear unintelligible voices here and there in the distance, communicating in laughing tones through the dark. All over the land human travelers hurry onward, seeking rest; birds jostle in the foliage; insects whine and click in the darkening fields; and the stars, getting brighter, sail over in their helpless multitudes.

As the familiar daytime aspects of things are gradually lost in the great fragrant darkness, the question of faith grows more distinct, more urgent, for we begin to perceive around us what *cannot* be relied on or revered as unchangeable and secure; namely, all of this that we can point to, label, and define, all conditioned, compounded things, however beautiful or alive with the evening's mystery. Earth, heavens, sentient beings, flowers in gardens, and all the swirl of worldly circumstance will not hold still and will not give lasting protection, nor last themselves. The invisible strands of spider web part on our skin as we walk, the stone hills infinitesimally crumble down the gullies, and the monumental forests themselves die and grow as mechanically as grass. Where in this ocean of time shall we rest? Nothing of a conditioned nature can finally satisfy the yearning mind. Beyond all present and escaping joys, we as conditioned beings aspire toward the unconditioned, toward liberation from all suffering. We require faith in what leads to that.

What a long walk this is, this tour of neighborhood and eternity. Material forms—of houses, trees, playgrounds, cars, and the rest—float by us on all sides, deprived of their weight and importance but in a way made more distinct by darkness; for we are now not so much beguiled by their incidental shapes and colors and instead begin to notice their sameness, their common liability to appear and disappear, their unsubstantiality, their transience in the transient world of perception. We glide among these forms, curiously akin, as around us the evening magically reveals something of the universal condition of things.

The theme of impermanence revisits us in the immediacy of nature, as our feet swing through cool grass, where still an unseen thorn will scratch us. Remembered words come back to us under the chatter of insects, telling of change and ripening in change as we walk and breathe. What, indeed, can we trust in among all the sparkling of sensation more than this underlying, elemental fact of change? We were teetering through sticks and weeds and bristling clumps of bushes, balancing on a crooked dirt path, but now we are in the open with hard ground beneath us. We wander down a half-seen sidewalk as the past and the places where we stood not ten minutes ago slide out of reach into memory. We pause wistfully at a dark cross-street in a slow current of air, waiting to savor some timeless, ethereal peace (as if it must descend when we determine to receive it!), but we notice still, even as the body hesitates, the endless leave-taking of the sensed moment. It fades, vanishes, and is succeeded by another moment of no stronger substance. So we step forward, we move on in eddies of sensation. Breath trickles in and puffs away. Legs stretch and stride, feet press and lift. A lit window up ahead mysteriously draws near, bobs past, and recedes. Lightning bugs with their discontinuous lights roam the lawns, while above us, scarcely visible in the last twilight, bats violently curve and cut. A child's laugh far away sounds faintly down the street. Just like this, lamented or prized, life passes.

And this, it seems, is all there is to life—these glimpses, sounds, and incidents continuously floating past. Faced with this melancholy flow, we have long sought in work, in possessions, in recreations, or in temporary passions some enduring importance, justification, or rightness. Determined to believe that the world is solid and capable of sustaining us, we stumble, astonished, through the tissue of its walls again and again, finding always more depth and disappointment. We complain and grieve until, it may be, by some rare fortune we hear the timeless Dhamma and begin to realize why all this unsatisfactoriness keeps happening. Despite our fears, no stony fate constrains us. No chaotic chance disposes of our life. It has always been a matter of causes and conditions, mostly unregarded, overlapping one another like wavelets falling ceaselessly upon the sand. So by long wearing the shape of our own shoreline has come to be and continues to change. Whatever the outward circumstances may be, whatever worldly factors wash against us, still the chief and overriding sculptor of our destiny is our own intentional action.

It may be that we do not understand our desires and purposes well or do not distinctly wish for this or that result, but nevertheless effects follow naturally from intentions that we act upon. Craving, fed by ignorance of the real nature of the universe, drives us to action—blundering action by which we try to govern the ungovernable and wrest substance from the unsubstantial. All this keeps failing, so suffering keeps arising. Laid out in the Buddha's teaching, the natural sequence is not hard to follow; the logic of suffering and the countervailing, bright logic of liberation unroll in his words until, if we listen rightly, we are inspired to look around with newborn intensity at this single moment of our existence, this summer instant fraught with change, and wonder if we can set our will to a better course.

Among the tumbling elements of mind, we find, there is always volition—the power to choose, the will to turn the current of our being toward either disaster or emancipation. But to what safe point on the clouded horizon shall we steer? It cannot be wise to seize on just any haphazard enthusiasm and go racing alone toward imagined fulfillment when trustworthy guidance is available. Volition, to be a power for happiness, must go paired with knowledge.

The momentum of nature—the business of rivers and clouds and stars running on and being ever renewed—gives cause for a primal faith in us, for a natural awe before the certainty of change; but do we not sense now also a certainty in wisdom passed down, in words that breathe and live because they truly reflect what breathes and lives? Long ago the Buddha, the Tathāgata, broke through the shimmering surfaces of the world, pierced the law of causality, and saw how things arise and pass away. Then selflessly, out of compassion, he taught the truths that lead to liberation from all suffering, showing the path to wanderers like us. As ages pass, dust fills the highways of the earth; rain washes monuments into sand; stars swarm and fly away; but this path holds true.

We have long marveled at nature's grand inertia, seeing ourselves as independent of it in proud moments and then as miserably helpless in times of gloom; but neither extreme view comprehends reality. We remain conditioned beings—we are shaped and changed continually by a multitude of changing factors—but we also possess this power of volition or will that, if it is wisely directed, can free us from the ignorant flood; and in the teaching of the Buddha we find the wise direction we need so badly. It is available and can be used not just as a set of theoretical explanations of the sensed universe but also as a means of deciding and acting honorably in daily life.

Although time in the largest sense may be limitless, although our wandering this evening gives us a feeling of space and freedom, still the choice of each moment matters for us temporary beings—whether to harass or to console, to cling or to let go, to push forward our imagined egos or to retire from contention, to contemplate or to ignore the signs of nature. Since consequences for us follow from our actions, we should not resign the construction of our future to unexamined, uncontrolled passions, feebly acknowledging the ignorant "I want" as the authority for any course of behavior. Rather we should see to it that when we act our actions flow out of a comprehensive, trustworthy philosophy about how the universe actually functions.

Buddhist faith, then, when aroused by listening and by contemplation, becomes not a purely emotional inclination but rather a calm and reasoned commitment—the considered, judicious application of our powers according to the best available guidance. If after study and reflection we come to see the teaching of the Buddha as beautiful, serene, profound, and promising, we simply cannot evade it, draw back, and deny its justice in our own life. That would be a failure of nerve as real and lamentable as in any other mortal challenge. If the Dhamma, the bright law of liberation, has indeed been well proclaimed by the Buddha and understood at least in principle by us, who now admit its power, then faith, in the sense of confidence, trust, and resolve, is both natural and fitting.

What makes the adoption of faith so difficult for us is that faith is not, as we perhaps have hoped, an automatic phenomenon, a spontaneous swell that is only to be awaited and ridden to safety. Faith, on the contrary, is an effort. Faith is an activity of the determined mind. Once we have seen a little and contemplated in the light of the Dhamma, and once we have admitted to ourselves that no lucky, external changes in the world will ever give us complete security, we must go ahead and exercise our own powers in spite of fear. We rightly wish to be sure of those doctrines by which we might commit to live; but how much certainty is required for wise and honorable action? And how can we demand to secure the end without the beginning? We cannot fairly expect to know enlightenment and *then* decide whether it is worthwhile trying to attain it, because enlightenment is the outcome of sustained work along the

Noble Eightfold Path. Here before us, thanks to the Buddha, is the path—its features described, its benefits made clear, its stages explained. If we would know its goal and if we would reach peace, it is surely time to travel and observe.

This evening we walk merely in a mechanical, material sense, feeling the slow swirl of summer air, moving this body across an ordinary suburban stretch of earth; but crossing the wasteland of ignorance will require more of us. If our breath now flows in eager exercise, if we are brought to attention by the shapes and suggestions of this mild, mysterious evening, that is good; we should realize that the Dhamma we have learned is illustrated in the impersonal stars, in the shadowy trees, in the lonely lights in windows, in the racing bats, in the dim redness of the western sky. We have received a gift of Dhamma from the Buddha, passed down through all these centuries of sorrow, and it illuminates what once was dark and fearful. This mortal body moves on through the pleasant evening—and this is a happy opportunity to observe—but mind goes farther, or can go farther, into astounding distances of insight, sailing on faith and knowledge toward a brighter country.

The whole evening will dissolve soon in sleep; and this very moment, this sparkling of sensation, is extinguished in the stream of things even as we seek to know it. Our attention must be sharper to perceive the present in its freshness, to note both internal and external things in more than a coarse, self-interested way. For manifestly we are not the only creatures who wander this evening, who pursue their desires and flee their fears through this bewildering universe. There are cicadas everywhere buzzing in the trees, insisting on their own existence as earnestly as we do. There is a cat over there, a ripple of darkness crossing a lawn—all wildness now, no longer a pet snoozing on a sofa but a predator seeking prey. And deep in the grass and bushes, we suspect, a silent clash of insects is still going on—a stiff, remorseless killing and chewing and consuming throughout all these acres of suburban peace. And out in the fields and woods we left behind, other creatures scamper and wait, pause and sniff, waiting to seize or to be seized, living tensely and dying unpitied in an agony in the dark. And all the while, above us in the scented and—to us—benign evening sky, bats on the hunt whip through breathtaking turns. Dream how we will, the world still trembles with dukkha; and when mindfulness at last begins to work, the fatuous romance of our hopes must be broken up by knowledge. This moment of walking and gazing and smelling unseen flowers is also a moment, we must see, of colossal and unremedied suffering.

When, back in the daylight, we emerged from our house, we felt the ceiling lift up, horizons fall away, and life expand to more commodious proportions. This, we thought, was good and promising. But now as the world grows bigger still, dispassionate attention shows us not only beauty but also menace and calamity. With an eye to things beyond our own temporary comfort, we see unease, incompleteness, and pain not as alien and extraneous dreams but as essential facts and components of all that stirs here in saṃsāra, the realm of birth and death. In these houses, in these rooms with lamps lit, we do not doubt there is, along with laughter, much fear and loneliness and anger and regret ranging desperately between the walls. Like cicadas we all insist, we cry out our desires; but sounds and wishes alike go out fading into the great night, merging into the ageless sigh of unsatisfactoriness.

Along the sidewalk still warm from the day, we pass like a bit of fluff momentarily detached from the urgency of life. A plaintive, unintelligible voice from a window seems now to signify and embody universal sorrow, and a brief rustling in a flower bed bespeaks unlimited fear and danger. Mosquitoes whining around our ears illustrate the nearness of affliction and yet remain mosquitoes still—facts and beings of a sensed moment. So symbols and realities mingle, reflecting back and forth the truth of things and making the Dhamma real for us.

We are tired this evening, but not so worn out by troubles that stars and cicadas and the scent of flowers cannot give us some mental ease. A mindful look helps to preserve us, it seems, from falling as we often do into brooding sorrow when we notice suffering. Yes, we must admit, the world changes, falters, and goes on seeking; but still what we perceive are ultimately only ownerless phenomena, empty formations that we need not grasp. We walk, these limbs move naturally in patterns, and all the neighborhood floats past simply as sights and sounds and smells and other ghosts of sensation.

Now, here before us in the whirring, clicking darkness is at last the house we live in—stark, unfamiliar, and impersonal now, merely a place, a grouping of conditions in a universe of conditions. Let us just stand before it a little while, peacefully contemplating what is happening here. A cricket somewhere near the front steps is chirping steadily, shrill and solitary under stars and maple trees and the dark, jutting outline of a roof. It could be singing in any age, in any wilderness; time does not matter to its longing, to its mechanical desiring in the slow-moving, indefinite evening. And above that roof, colored lights of a distant airplane pass slowly and silently across the sky, while music from somewhere down the street plays at the edge of hearing—merely a beat and a sigh of unclear tones rising and dropping away.

Here is a pattern of elements endlessly unraveling and spinning together and rising up again. And here among them are a hand and a foot and a breath felt as a small stretching of muscles. Here are impermanent things wavering in and out of existence. Eyes receive what light there is; ears go on admitting sounds; nose detects the scents of gardens; skin registers the slow cooling of the atmosphere all around. Ideas bloom and blend and vanish. Names, notions, moods, and memories arise and disperse, too, as various as the twittering, unseen insects, until it seems that all of life is airy and weightless, scarcely tethered to anything.

Change shudders through all phenomena, but must we always clutch at them? Suffering exists, but has it not an origin and a cessation as well? And through actions well chosen might it not be destroyed? We find no self in any of the evening's shadows—might we not abandon that exhausted dream? What strange, clear thoughts these are! We have heard them before and now they come back fresh, as if newly spoken in our wakeful ears. Perhaps we will not retire just yet, for the landscape is full of meanings. Let us look around as well as we can and learn good truth. Other eyes than ours have measured this ardent, flowering world, and other minds have known it better. The Buddha was here long before us, seeing and understanding and speaking out of compassion—he who was undeceived by beauty, undaunted by pain, the giver of what is good and worthy. The Buddha was here—is here still, embodied in the Dhamma that now shines around us steadier than the starlight.

A cricket goes on calling and calling as we gaze outward over the trees. Where in this wild universe shall we stand without fear? Where among all opinions and dreams shall we plant our faith? The night receives in silence the cricket's call and our own speechless questions.

Whom shall we believe? The earth is dark and speaks no word, but for all the depth and dizziness of space, for all the confusion flooding down through time, one thing, at least, we know.

About Wisdom Publications

WISDOM PUBLICATIONS, a nonprofit publisher, is dedicated to making available authentic works relating to Buddhism for the benefit of all. We publish books by ancient and modern masters in all traditions of Buddhism, translations of important texts, and original scholarship. Additionally, we offer books that explore East-West themes unfolding as traditional Buddhism encounters our modern culture in all its aspects. Our titles are published with the appreciation of Buddhism as a living philosophy, and with the special commitment to preserve and transmit important works from Buddhism's many traditions.

To learn more about Wisdom, or to browse books online, visit our website at www.wisdompubs.org.

You may request a copy of our catalog online or by writing to this address:

Wisdom Publications
199 Elm Street
Somerville, Massachusetts 02144 USA
Telephone: 617-776-7416
Fax: 617-776-7841
Email: info@wisdompubs.org
www.wisdompubs.org

The Wisdom Trust

AS A NONPROFIT PUBLISHER, Wisdom is dedicated to the publication of Dharma books for the benefit of all sentient beings and dependent upon the kindness and generosity of sponsors in order to do so. If you would like to make a donation to Wisdom, you may do so through our website or our Somerville office. If you would like to help sponsor the publication of a book, please write or email us at the address above.
Thank you.

Wisdom is a nonprofit, charitable 501(c)(3) organization affiliated with the Foundation for the Preservation of the Mahayana Tradition (FPMT).

Landscapes of Wonder
Discovering Buddhist Dharma in the World Around Us
Bhikkhu Nyanasobhano
192 pages, ISBN 0-86171-142-4, $14.95

"Highly recommended...written in a magical kind of prose."—*Library Journal*

"The writing is often grandly inspiring.... Nyanasobhano's often exhilarating prose makes for a moving and memorable book."—*Publishers Weekly*

"American Buddhism has at last found its Thoreau. This is an eloquent, joyous, and uplifting book, written with consummate skill."—Bhikkhu Bodhi, editor and translator of *In the Buddha's Words*

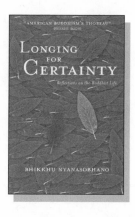

Longing for Certainty
Reflections on the Buddhist Life
Bhikkhu Nyanasobhano
256 pages, ISBN 0-86171-338-9, $14.95

"This volume sets itself apart as an unusually practical, philosophical, and graceful book, brimming with the stuff of everyday life, and elegantly laced with poetry. This is a volume to be treasured and re-read by Buddhists of all types and stages, as well as non-Buddhists who love nature and are curious about a path that winds toward home. Deep and shining."—*Publishers Weekly*

"Bhikkhu Nyanasobhano sets out to explain Buddhist principles as they present themselves in everyday life. He has a knack for using ordinary incidents to elucidate complex Buddhist ideas and ideals."—*Spirituality and Health*

"Nature lovers will find a companion for the trail in *Longing for Certainty*. Bhikkhu Nyanasobhano blends depictions of idyllic landscapes with scriptural quotes in a series of musings on life. The simple message of this book is appealing: the author encourages the reader to find the Buddhist teachings in everyday life and especially the natural world."—*Buddhadharma*